The better days
Are few and far between
But I've come
So far
From where I've been

Preface

I went to psychiatric hospital... for ten weeks. For some family and friends this is old news, but for most this is the first they're hearing about it. The reason for that is because I'm ashamed of my struggles with my mental health, and wanted to disclose this on a strictly need to know basis. But, ironically, I'm ashamed of being ashamed, because I have learnt and benefited so much from those brave enough to share their story. If we want the stigma surrounding mental illness to be reduced, then it will take people sharing insight and helping others to understand their experiences. At first, this was a private project as part of my therapy, as I didn't want anyone to know this part of me. But this only maintains the mask and walls I have hidden behind for years. However, when I reflected on how much I gained from stories like mine, I decided to put my pride aside on the off chance my experience and story has a similar impact. I'm not claiming to have all the answers, and I recognise in shame my hypocrisy of not following half the advice in these pages. But if I can help just one person, to inspire them to seek help, motivate them to keep going, or just help increase the empathy given to a struggling loved one, then the discomfort of sharing the darkest moments in the depths of my illness, will be more than worth it. At the time of writing, I am out of hospital but still unwell and having regular therapy. But this means I have lost my ability to recognise thoughts, feelings, and behaviours that can upset others. So I am sharing content that may be distressing, my sincere apologies for that. My time in hospital was the most terrifying and enlightening time, and vital to my journey. There are some things only I and psychiatric professionals will ever know. So, for now, here are the parts I'm willing to share.

3

' There is hope, even when your brain tells you there isn't '

John Green

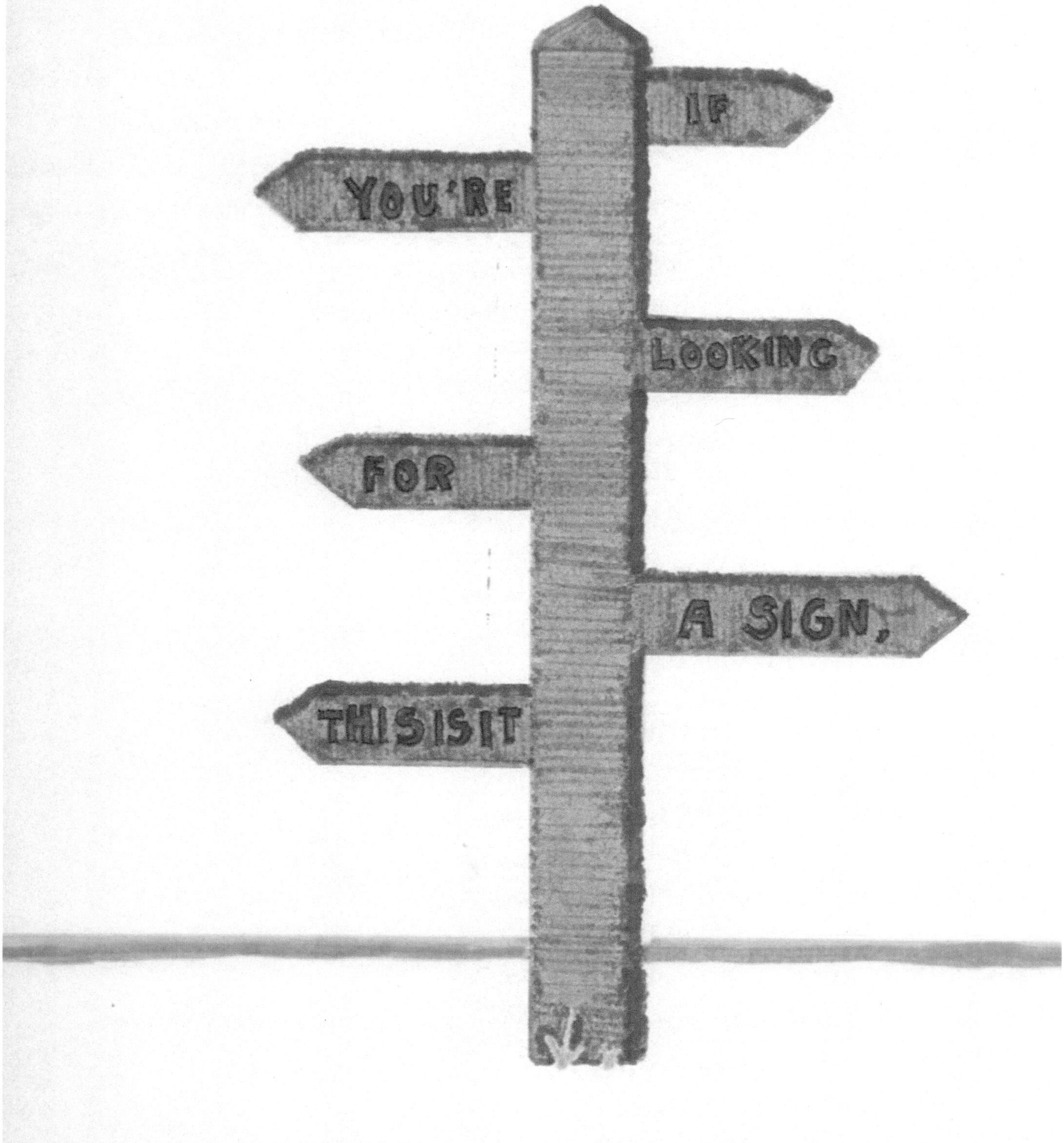
IF
YOU'RE
LOOKING
FOR
A SIGN,
THIS IS IT

Just as no two people are exactly alike, no two people experience mental illness in the same way. These are the main symptoms I experience. The thoughts, feelings, physical manifestations, and behaviour.

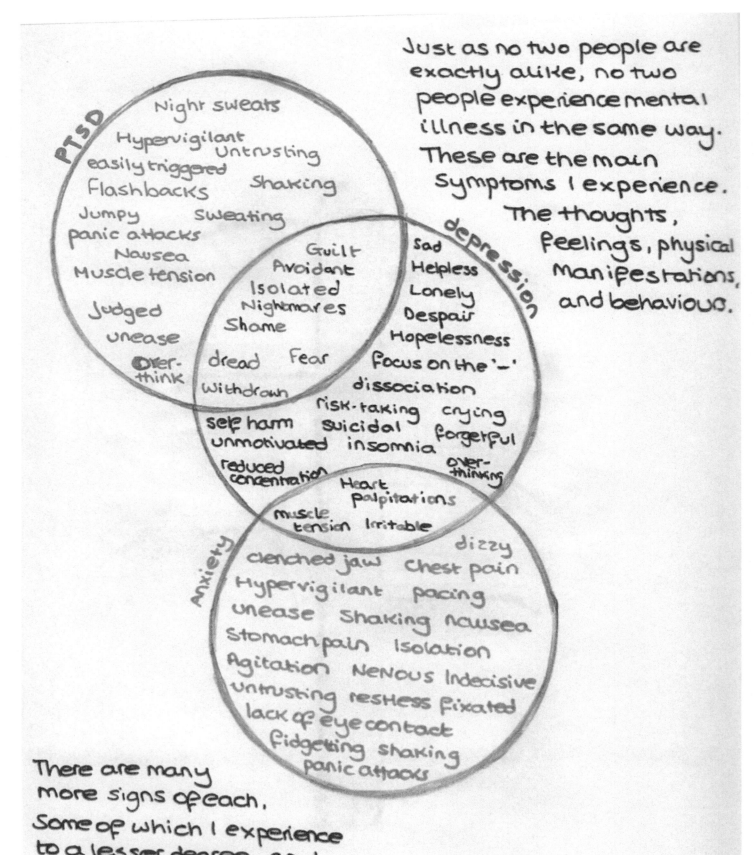

PTSD
Night sweats
Hypervigilant
Untrusting
easily triggered
Flashbacks
Shaking
Jumpy
Sweating
panic attacks
Nausea
Muscle tension
Judged
Unease
Over-think

Guilt
Avoidant
Isolated
Nightmares
Shame
dread   Fear
Withdrawn
risk-taking
self harm   suicidal
unmotivated   insomnia
reduced concentration

depression
Sad
Helpless
Lonely
Despair
Hopelessness
Focus on the '—'
dissociation
crying
forgetful
over-thinking

Heart palpitations
muscle tension   Irritable

Anxiety
clenched jaw   dizzy
Chest pain
Hypervigilant   pacing
Unease   Shaking   nausea
Stomach pain   Isolation
Agitation   Nervous   Indecisive
Untrusting   restless   Fixated
lack of eye contact
fidgeting   shaking
panic attacks

There are many more signs of each, some of which I experience to a lesser degree, and a few that I have not. This may not be an exhaustive list, but each and every symptom is certainly exhausting.

'Quiet people
have the loudest
minds'
-Stephen King

Journaling and mood tracking ideas

— · — MOOD — · · —

	Sad	happy	anxious	angry	tired
M	o	o	o	o	o
T	o	o	o	o	o
W	o	o	o	o	o
T	o	o	o	o	o
F	o	o	o	o	o
S	o	o	o	o	o
S	o	o	o	o	o

『 What am I grateful for? 』

┌ Physical exercise and activity ┐

minutes	M T W T F S S

✶ Sleep tracking ✶

PM 12 1 2 3 4 5 6 7 8 9 10 11 AM 12 1 2 3 4 5 6 7 8 9 10 11

M T W T F S S

Wellbeing

	M T W T F S S
Exercise	o o o o o o o
Socialising	o o o o o o o
Healthy eating	o o o o o o o
Working	o o o o o o o
Hobbies	o o o o o o o

	M T W T F S S
cleaning	o o o o o o o
Social media	o o o o o o o
relaxation	o o o o o o o
8+hrs sleep	o o o o o o o
Hydration	o o o o o o o

My First night in hospital

Tears. That's the immediate memory. Collected from the waiting room by a nurse from the ward I was assigned to. The tears ran down my cheeks as I hugged my family goodbye, and was escorted to the ward. I had no idea what to expect from my admission to hospital, or how long I would be there. The door to my room was unlocked, and swung open to reveal a "safe room". No ligature points, no rails or hangers in the wardrobe, no door handles, a two direction door with a window to the corridor. 'I've made a mistake, I want to go home' was my initial, fear ladened thought as my bag was emptied and searched. The crying persisted throughout. All risky items were placed in a locker : my phone charger, my perfume (due to the glass bottle), my tweezers, and also almost my teddy. My emotionally infantile mind needs the comfort of a teddy at times like this, so the consideration of it being cut open in case it contained any restricted items broke me. But I was granted my teddy, fully intact. I stopped crying during the health assessment in the clinic room, only I believe due to complete emotional exhaustion. After measuring my height, weight, blood pressure, an ECG, blood test, and urine sample, I was entirely overwhelmed.

I was taken to dinner, despite my complete absence of appetite due to anxious nausea. I sat alone at one of the long tables, my left finger tips on my forehead, tears dripping onto my untouched plate. I forced down a few mouthfuls, then cleared my plate to stack on the side. It was still early evening but I just wanted to sleep. The distress had drained all my energy and I didn't want to be conscious anymore. So, despite the warmth of the April evening, I wrapped myself in my dressing gown, with the hood up, so it smelled like home. I crawled into bed, folded into a ball, with my teddy against my chest, and cried myself to sleep.

EMOTIONS

- dealing with:
  - anger
  - sadness
  - anxiety
  - lonliness

- emotional regulation

- Fear

ANGER

Types

Aggressive
- Inappropriate
- controlling / attacking

Passive
- indirect
- internalised
- avoidant

Assertive
- appropriate
- honest
- empathic
- constructive

Passive-aggressive
- dishonest
- manipulative
- emotion based
- hurtful

Responses

- physical or verbal attacks. Deliberately hurtful.
- difficulty with self-control
- persistent feelings of anger
- quick to respond angrily
- making assumptions
- regret about past actions or words
- headache
- blaming

Managing anger

- Reminding yourself
  - to not need to control the situation
  - to check the facts
  - trusting the ability of others
  - to reflect on the cause and how to overcome the issue
  - to practice assertiveness
  - to focus on the positives

Positive self-talk

- I am able to control my emotions
- I won't let this negatively impact me
- It is okay to be angry but I need to control it
- Is this worth feeling like this?
- What would I rather be happening right now? can I do anything to make that happen?

Underneath anger

Anger can be a response to other emotions, such as:

- Anxiety
- Fear
- Embarrasment
- Hurt
- Shame
- Betrayed
- Sadness
- Jealousy
- loneliness
- rejection
- Shock
- Frustration
- violation
- confusion
- Guilt

SADNESS

Signs and symptoms:
- short-term upset
- fatigue
- crying
- seeking comfort
- irritable
- discouraged
- >2 weeks could be depression

coping with sadness:
- acknowledge the situation
- be gentle with yourself
- connect with others
- exercise
- allow yourself to be sad
- process the emotion
- seek help if needed

'your sadness is a gift. Don't reject it. Don't rush it. live it fully and use it as fuel to change and grow'

- maxime Legacé

what is stronger than the human heart which shatters over and over and still lives

- Rupi Kaur

Potential causes:
- relationship issues
- loss / grief
- illness (self or loved one)
- world events
- long-term injury
- change
- bullying

possible outcomes:
- feeling okay again
- denial
- depression
- acceptance
- resilience
- anger
- internalised emotion
- anxiety

ANXIETY

'One of the most frustrating things about having an anxiety disorder; knowing as you are freaking out that there's no reason to be freaked out, but lacking the ability to shut the emotion down.'

— unknown

Habits that can make anxiety worse:

- Avoidance
- Over-use of social media
- needing control
- poor physical health
- lack of sleep
- caffeine, alcohol and other substances
- comparing yourself
- overworking

'Living with anxiety is like being followed by a voice. It knows all your insecurities and uses them against you. It gets to the point when it's the loudest voice in the room. The only one you can hear.'

— unknown

Affirmations:

I can release control

I can accept what I cannot change

I am stronger than my feelings

I give myself permission to move on

I'm not my thoughts. They don't define me

Anxiety makes it hard to:

- Keep relationships
- Travel
- Talk to superiors
- Take phone calls
- Be organised
- Do new things
- Relax
- Cope with change
- open up
- Start conversation

'A panic attack goes from 0 to 100 in an instant. It's halfway between feeling like you'll faint and feeling like you'll die!'

— unknown

Managing anxiety:

- implementing routine
- practice rational / factual thinking
- mindfulness
- journalling
- seeking help if needed
- preparation (but not too much!)
- establish boundaries
- develop a support system
- Remind yourself that:
  - ↳ you are capable
  - ↳ you've coped before
  - ↳ the feeling will pass
  - ↳ I am safe

14

LONLINESS

Types

- Emotional
  ↳ Social isolation
- Situational
  ↳ difficult environment or relationship
- Social
  ↳ communication issues
- chronic

Signs

Fatigue   Small number of close friends   insomnia

Increased frequency of sickness

feeling isolated   self-doubt

poor concentration   development of mental illness

anxious   helplessness

'The wind breathes lonely,
longing to be seen.
Sometimes, the soul has
days like these.'

Angie Weiland-Crosby

overcoming loneliness

- understanding yourself in order to find people or groups to interact with
  ↳ personality e.g. shy, or extrovert
  ↳ hobbies and interests
  ↳ your career, home town, relationship, dreams/goals

- Re-consider how to spend free time
- Join online groups, forums etc.
- meet people in person
- Practice thinking positively, conversation skills, how to meet new people, maintaining relationships. or other useful tools

Emotional Regulation

Notice the emotion

Allow and release the emotion Validate yourself.

Name and describe the emotion

Investigate the emotion. How does it feel in my body? Where has it come from?

Accept and don't judge the emotion

If healthy and safe to do so, meeting the needs of the intense emotion can help to alleviate its strength. Learning to sit with the emotion and allow it to pass can greatly help in the management of strong emotions.

opposite action

- The alternative to meeting the emotion's need, if that is inappropriate or unhealthy
- This can help to understand, de-escalate, and manage the emotion
- Acknowledging the emotion and actively being more productive and effective

check the facts

- assumptions can lead to overreactions and an unnecessary suffering
- Rationally working through the emotion to reduce the intensity or identify the importance of the trigger
- Does your response match the context?

preventing intense emotion

Get enough **S** leep

T ake care of yourself

R esist negative behaviours

E xercise

N utrition

G ain mastery. Focus on what you can control

T ake time for yourself

H ealthy self-talk

S.T.R.E.N.G.T.H

Common Causes

- Anxiety
- Phobias
- Trauma
- Injury
- Illness
- Loss
- Memories
- change
- seperation anxiety
- Future
- Imagination
- Danger
- The unknown
- Threat

Symptoms

- sweating
- Trembling
- chills or hot flushes
- heart racing
- Shortness of breath
- chest pain
- lightheadedness
- avoidance

Fear

Managing fear

Acknowledge and name it
↓
describe it ———→ Analyse the potential good and bad of the situation
↓
find possible solutions
↓
use skills to cope if unavoidable

Develop skills to cope with...
- failure
- judgement
- embarrasment
- change
- Other causes of fear

'Courage is the resistance to fear, mastery of fear, not absence of fear'
- Mark Twain

'Success is not final. Fear is not fatal. It is the courage to continue that counts.'
- Winston churchill

LEADING MENTAL
HEALTH PROBLEMS
WORLDWIDE:

1 Depression

2 Anxiety disorders   } Positions regularly swap

3 Bipolar disorder

4 Eating disorders

(our world in data, 2022)
(WHO, 2022)

¾ of mental illnesses are established by age 24

- ~280 million people suffer from depression worldwide

- suicide was the 4th leading cause of death among 15-29 year olds in 2019
  ⌐ ONS, 2014

- Data from official reports of domestic violence, which is strongly linked to mental health difficulties, states that 1·2 million women and 700,000 men were victims

(World Health Organisation, 2021)
(Global Health Data Exchange, '21)

Startling Stats

Black, Asian, and minority ethnic communities:

- Black men are more likely to experience mental health problems than white men

- impacts on mental health in BAME communities
  - discrimination
  - social and economic inequality
  - stigma
  - racism

LGBTQ+ people:

- ½ of LGBTQ+ people have experienced depression

- 1 in 8 LGBTQ+ people aged 18 to 24 have attempted suicide

- Hate crime and fear of discrimination impacts mental health and access to support

- A study in 2007 found that individuals with learning difficulties are 54% more likely to suffer from mental health problems

- Almost 1 in 4 young women have a mental illness (BBC, 2018)

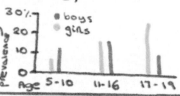

■ boys
● girls

30%
20
10
0
Prevalence
Age 5-10   11-16   17-19

Seek the help you deserve

National Suicide prevention helpline
0800 689 5652

Samaritans
116 123

SANEline
0300 304 7000

SHOUT
text 'SHOUT' to 85258

If you're under 35

Papyrus Hopeline
0800 068 4141

For LGBT individuals

Switchboard
0300 330 0630

mind.org.uk
papyrus-uk.org
Samaritans.org
nhs.uk   nimh.nih.gov
mentalhealth.org
sprc.org

VALIDATION

Make yourself
a priority

At the end of
the day, you
are your longest
commitment

Be gentle with
yourself
You're doing the
best you can

Do not feel guilty for prioritising your mental health	You are stronger than you think	Embrace change. Even the smallest of steps is still progress.	Mistakes are proof that you are trying

Life
Is
Tough,
but
so
are
you

'One day you
will tell your story
of how you
overcame what you
went through and
it will be someone
else's survival guide'
Brene Brown

REMINDERS

You cannot control the storm.

But you can learn to sail

Dialectical Behavioural Therapy

Therapy consists of :
- interpersonal relationships
- Emotion regulation
- Distress tolerance
- Mindfulness

evidence-based psychotherapy based on CBT, designed to treat individuals who experience intense emotions and harmful coping strategies

Involves group therapy

Originally developed as a therapy for borderline personality disorder

Cognitive Behavioural Therapy

psychotherapy that is based on the idea that thoughts, beliefs and attitudes impact feelings and behaviours

Therapy consists of identifying and reorganising unhelpful and negative thoughts and beliefs

developing more positive behavioural patterns can also impact thoughts

The key basis of Cognitive Behavioural Therapy is:

What you think and do impacts how you feel

Thoughts ← → Emotions
Body sensations ← → Behaviours

making changes to thinking and behaviours to improve how you feel. Requires active participation.

Healthy life balance

ACE

- **A**chieve   - **C**onnect   - **E**njoy

To maintain wellbeing and biology changes to improve mental wellness

- Achievement → dopamine
- Connection → oxytocin
- Purpose → serotonin
- Exercise → endorphins

Planning and journaling encourages keeping time to carry these out. and then reflect on the effects.

CBT Skills

Challenging thinking errors

- Is there evidence?
- Am I generalising, jumping to conclusions, or assuming?
- Am I expecting too much?
- What are the pros and cons?
- Am I concentrating on the negatives?

Recognising worry

- circular thoughts or conversations in your head
- questions with no answers or 'what if' questions

Rigid expectations

- I or they should / must / have to and if not then...

- Is my thought a factor opinion?
  ↳ either way, don't judge yourself or the thought. it has come from somewhere

- Tolerating uncertainty
  ↳ question whether it is beneficial, and what the cost of the uncertainty is.
  ↳ focus on what you can control

- worry thought record
  - Situation, date and time
  - what is my worry?
  - what am I predicting?
  - Name the emotion and its intensity (%)
  - Is there evidence for my prediction? and against?
  - How likely is it to occur?

Dialectical Behaviour Therapy : Skills

Dialectical thinking

- Maintaining an openness to contradictory and/or polarised thoughts, behaviours, and points of view.
- Combining these to form a "truth" that best explains the reality of the moment
- Consider both perspectives

Emotion regulation

- Understanding the emotional experience
- Decrease vulnerability and emotional suffering
- Accumulate short and long term positives

Interpersonal effectiveness

Describe Express Assert Reinforce	working for what you want/need	Mindful Appear confident Negotiate

Mindfulness

Use skills with:

Awareness
Acceptance
Action

one-mindful

- One thing at a time
- Notice any distractions, and let them go

Observe, describe, and participate

↳ notice just the facts, without judgement

Wise mind

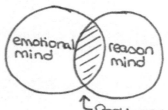

↑ Feelings + knowledge work together with intuition

- MASTERY

  Mindful of the emotion,
  Act opposite to the emotion,
  Self validation, Turn the mind
  Experience building positives
  Radical acceptance

Gentle Interested Validate Easy manner	
Fair Apology-free Stick to values Truthfulness	gaining and maintaining relationships

Distress tolerance

See page

- Radical acceptance
- crisis survival skills
- self soothe
- STOP
- TIPP

Overthinking.

Overthinking steals
you away from the
present moment. Give
yourself permission to live
without over analysing
your behaviour. Release
yourself from the shackles
of your mind that keep
you trapped in a cycle
of self-doubt and skepticism.

– Ash Alves

Typical ways of diagnosing mental illness

A diagnosis can be a really helpful insight that can be a source of reassurance and a starting point for appropriate and relevant treatment

Medical professional will assess:
- Your experience
  - Feelings
  - behaviours
  - physical symptoms
- How long you have been experiencing the symptoms
- The impact on your daily life

- These details can be given through questionnaires or a conversation
- If symptoms alter over time, it is possible the diagnosis can change
- A diagnosis does not necessarily mean intervention is needed, but a regular review can help to indicate whether further support is required
- A GP is able to diagnose mental health problems but may also refer to a mental health specialist
- Remember : a diagnosis does not define you, and is only a small portion of who you are as an individual

What is
Worrying
me most
at the
moment?

Have I
settled
for less
than I
deserve?

Is there a
pattern to
my negative
thinking or
behaviour?

What could
I be doing
more/less
of to
feel better?

What
would I
tell my
younger
self?

How am
I when
I am
alone?

Am I lying
to myself
about
anything?

How do I
know when
I am doing
okay, or
not?

What am
I proud
of myself
for right now?

Ask Yourself

28

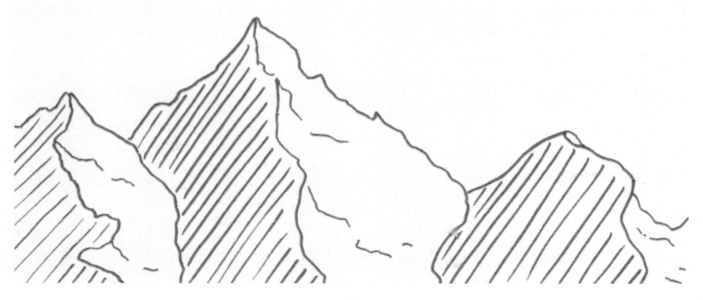

STARS SHINE BRIGHTEST IN THE DARKEST OF SKIES

depression is
♥ Love ♥

Well, no, it isn't. But a thought occured to me, that they are not that different. You could make very similar statements about both. Yet, one is far more accepted and "real" compared to the other. Love is just as invisible and yet we not only talk about it more, but have so many songs, movies, even a day dedicated to it. But, love is, in it's most basic form, just an idea. A concept so strong that millions seek it, become consumed by it. However, love can also be difficult, occasionally harmful. Love can be forbidden, unrequited, lost, manipulated; But so many take the risk regardless. Depression, granted is primarily negative, can be / is experienced in unique ways. Just like love, it can manifest as biological, emotional, and physical symptoms. They are both just concepts based on their features, and are different in every person. So if we can have some understanding of love, despite not being able to "see" it directly, can we not do the same for depression? We have such a comparatively limited grasp on what depression is, despite the extent of its presence in society, the suffering it inflicts. and the ultimately lethal potential it has. This lack of knowledge maintains the stigma and fear around it. Depression cannot be seen explicitly, hence the widespread denial that if we pretend it isn't really there then it will be okay. I can sympathise with this; it is painful to acknowledge that this invisible, silent killer could inflict harm on any one of us, our loved ones, with no real protection. But we must. It is time we admit that it is very much a real thing, though we cannot see it. It is time we thought about it like love...

It is normal	We must keep people safe with it	Share experiences	encourage openness	It is invisible but do not
It is not your fault		Give support when things go wrong	everyone experiences it differently	disregard it, it is there

journal extracts

I have used journaling, admittedly on quite an inconsistent basis, throughout the years of struggling with my mental health. It is now something I use daily, to draw attention to what is playing on my mind. Sometimes having to put a feeling or emotion into words can provide some clarity, but primarily it is a process of simply letting go of all the hurt inside.

I have not included specific events, and I haven't disclosed any names. The past and certain experiences will remain confidential, as secrets only known by mental health professionals and myself. Instead, I have provided an insight into the unrelenting and malicious thought processes haunt my mind. I am aware this may therefore make for upsetting reading; but an unapologetically truthful account of my reality will hopefully encourage a greater understanding of the ruthless power of an unsettled mind.

I am able to appreciate my loss of objectivity and detatchment from the subject matter. This may mean that some of the extracts that I now read with indifference, are actually rather distressing. For this I apologise, but if you lived with these thoughts and emotions I am almost certain you would lose some perspective too. And if you are unable to relate to what I write, I am very jealous.

2014 - 2017

The early parts of my journaling, which detail the mind of a distressed teenager, I still find to be generally relatable. This provides a harsh reminder that, 10 years on almost, I have made very little progress with my mental state. Though demoralising, I can now see some patterns that I previously did not, thanks to the knowledge I am gradually gaining from therapy. So that's something.

I'm tired. But I don't want to sleep because that means having to wake up and survive another day

I don't even notice I'm sad anymore. It's just become a part of who I am.

I'm so done with feeling like this.

I'm scared of telling people how much I'm hurting

Never, ever, tell a suicidal person they 'won't do it' because I can guarantee they will want to prove you wrong

It hurt when you said you thought that I just 'can't be bothered' to stay alive. I really thought you understood more than that.

Where is there to go when all I want to do is run away from myself

Please stop being angry. I have no control over this.

How do I manage to fuck up everything I do...?

I wish I could take away all the times I let you kiss me. I wish we had never met.

I have so much love to give and no one to give it to. Not even myself

I wish no one knew I was unwell. Then I could just go. By "accident" so there was no guilt or blame.

Either prove to me what you're saying is true, or just stop messing me around

Nope. I'm scared.

There's so much almost everyone doesn't know about me

I wish I could pause my life until I feel better. I'm too young for this shit. These should be the best years of my life. I want to live. Not just survive.

Why can't I function like a normal person?!

You never understand. But the worst part is that you don't even try to.

You really don't fucking get it

I hear such weird shit that's not even there

Are you ashamed of me?

No one seems to get how hard all this is

It's bad again.

Do you do this on purpose?

34

I'm fed up of wearing long sleeves. Its too hot.

I've come to realise there are very few people I can actually rely on

I can't do this. I want to cut so deep I don't feel the pain anymore

please will you love me?

I'm either numb or in pain. why is there nothing inbetween?

I need a hug

I'm secretly really scared

If only I was as happy as I pretend I am. Don't be fooled, I'm not as okay as I let on.

I am very very scared. How does no one understand that?

Saying 'I'm fine' is 100 x easier than explaining why I'm sad

Do I keep lying, telling people I'm okay, and making up excuses? Or do I tell the truth?

Yes I feel sorry for myself sometimes, but only because I feel like the only one thats cares

Please just show me you care

I haven't cried for a while. A while being 24 or so hours. I'm too exhausted, and crying does fuck all.

How did I let you win...

Showering hides the tears

I trusted you.

You don't give a shit about me

If you won't let me kill myself, at least allow me to hurt myself. Please don't take that away from me.

If only I had done things differently

Please help me. I'm scared.

I know I can't take a joke. I am one.

I constantly decide between not cutting and cutting deeper

Please, I need you

What did I ever do to deserve you?

I will, at some point, let you down

My comfort blanket is a blade

I always feel in trouble when I'm telling someone how bad I feel

I look at other people's arms to see if they have scars too.

Get out of my life. How can you treat me like this, and then blame and guilt trip me?! How dare you. Fuck off. Fuck you.

Will anyone ever listen?

How much pain do I have to go through until giving up is okay?

You said that if I killed myself you'd never get over it. Then please please help me. I don't know what else to do to make it stop.

"But are you even trying to get better?"
Please don't ask me that, I will only disappoint you. I gave up on everything a long time ago, what's the point in getting better? The world is a horrible place full of people doing horrible things

Trying to tell people with no experience of mental illness why I can't go out because I feel unwell is so hard. They think I'm rude, lazy, lying, or worse that I don't care about them. But in reality I'm desperate to see them, my mind is keeping me away from everyone and everything I love.

36

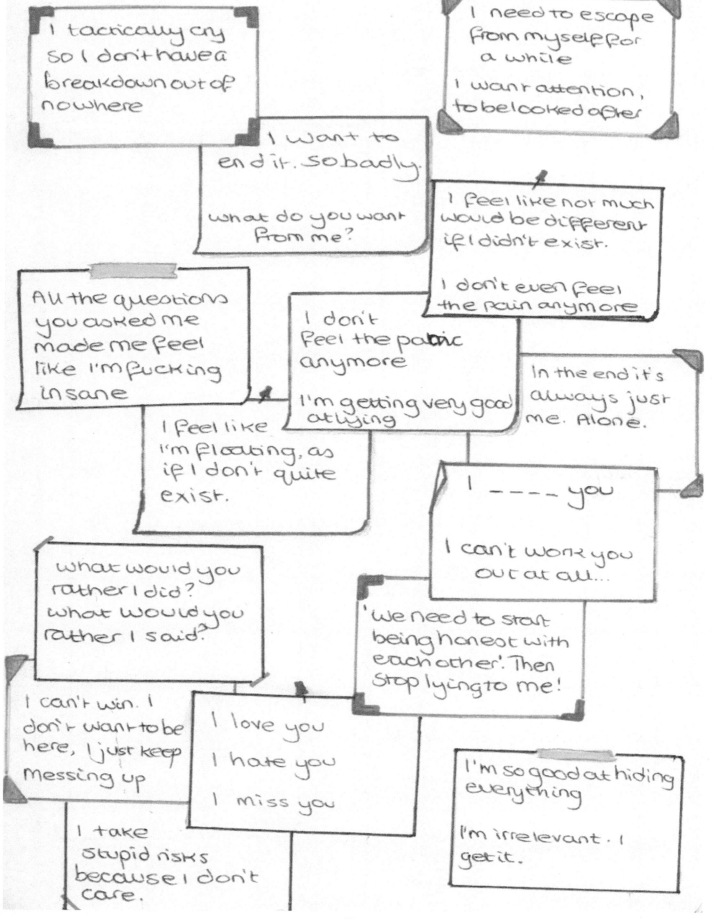

I'm sorry
I annoy you

I'm sorry
I waste your time

I'm sorry
I didn't listen

I'm sorry
you didn't think I
was trying

I'm sorry
I've let you down

You can tell me a hundred times but I won't believe you. i've been lied to too many times before. I don't trust anymore.

I'm addicted to hurting myself

I'm never happy, just less sad

I hate being okay. Okay is not good, but isn't bad enough for anyone to care.

I'm too exhausted to cry.

I'm so tired of all this shit.

I messed up. Again.

Don't cry in front of them. Please fight back the tears. Please, just don't let them see me cry.

It's okay that you've given up on me. I gave up on myself and everyone else a long time ago. So, I get it.

I feel so alone. All. The. Time.

my best wasn't good enough. I get it.

Do not start self harming. If you do, you won't ever stop thinking about it. Trust me.

I've got so good at pretending I'm okay that it surprises everyone when I break down. I act like I'm fine. But I hurt so much inside.

everyone else gave up on me. So why can't I?

I'm so scared of you

Some days I dream of the future. Other days I dream of how to prevent it.

my mood swings terrify me. They come out of no where

you compared your cold to my depression. That's not okay. Your cold will go. It doesn't make you want to die just to make it stop. You don't have to see doctors, psychiatrists, therapists. People help you, they don't awkwardly avoid your illness. They understand its not your fault. You don't feel completely alone. I don't want pity, just understanding and awareness. This is terrifying, it's exhausting, it's relentless.

I've written my note to you. Only you. You're the only one to take the time to understand and support me.

I was getting better...

How can you STILL not see how much I'm struggling?

I hate myself. A lot.

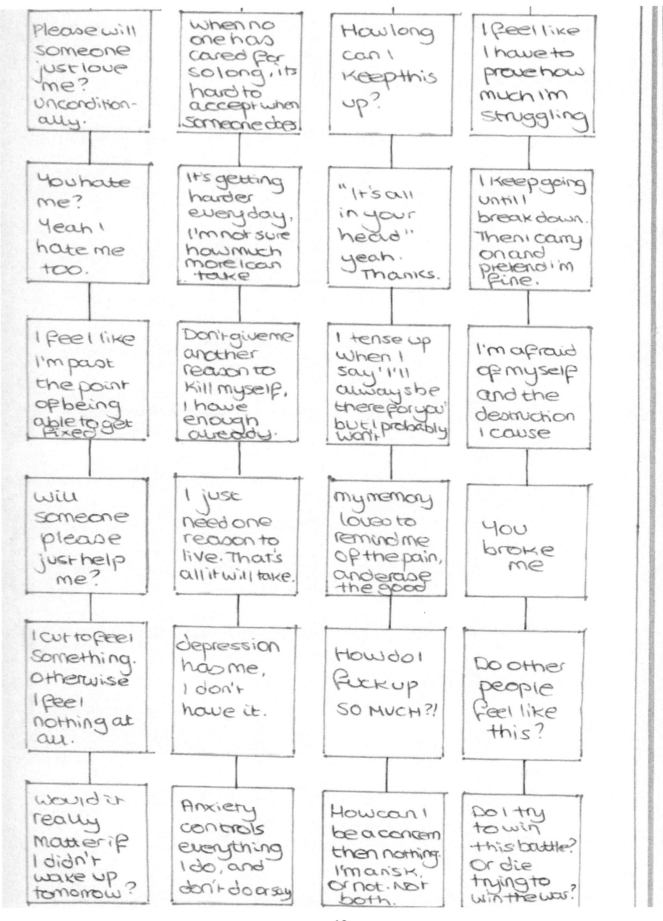

Please will someone just love me? Unconditionally.

when no one has cared for so long, it's hard to accept when someone does.

How long can I keep this up?

I feel like I have to prove how much I'm struggling

You hate me? Yeah I hate me too.

It's getting harder everyday, I'm not sure how much more I can take

"It's all in your head" yeah. Thanks.

I keep going until I break down. Then I carry on and pretend I'm fine.

I feel like I'm past the point of being able to get fixed

Don't give me another reason to kill myself, I have enough already.

I tense up when I say 'I'll always be there for you' but I probably won't

I'm afraid of myself and the destruction I cause

Will someone please just help me?

I just need one reason to live. That's all it will take.

my memory loves to remind me of the pain, and erase the good

You broke me

I cut to feel something. Otherwise I feel nothing at all.

depression has me, I don't have it.

How do I fuck up so much?!

Do other people feel like this?

Would it really matter if I didn't wake up tomorrow?

Anxiety controls everything I do, and don't do or say

How can I be a concern then nothing. I'm a risk, or not. Not both.

Do I try to win this battle? Or die trying to win the war?

I'm scared, alone, and confused by what is happening to me

The idea of just coping and struggling for the rest of my life sounds shit. I don't want that for my future.

I need time to write how I feel, I am completely overwhelmed if I have to verbalise it

I want to be looked after

I feel misunderstood but its my fault because i pretend to be okay. But only because i can't share how I feel in this environment.

Life overwhelms me.

I'm trying so hard to get better, but its painful and takes time. Time that I feel has run out.

I'm disappointing everyone

I don't trust anyone not to hurt me. Physically or mentally.

suicide genuinely feels like a better option than suffering for the benefit of everyone else

I've been fighting alone for so long

having the emotional state of a child makes adulthood so hard to navigate

I feel so weak and pathetic

I'm just trying to protect you

I feel like I annoy people just by being here

I can feel my body shutting down when I get really sad or scared. It gives up with my mind.

I was forced into independence but now I feel so alone

I numb myself so often. I don't want to feel all this.

Love scares me. It acts as a perfect mask for evil

I don't think I actually know what happiness is

Sleep is so good. It provides a break from the headache from holding back tears, thinking, re-thinking, and over-thinking.

How am I expected to cope
all alone when I get home?

People love to use me and my life against me, and
I don't know how to argue against that. But there is
very little about a person that can protect them from
developing mental illness.

My brain hurts. Its more than a headache, its a dull
pounding deep within my skull. I understand all the
logic of life, but thinking about all the
other aspects sends my brain into overdrive.
Feelings, emotions, thoughts, memories, fears,
and flashbacks are all too much for me.

If I was this close to death from a physical
illness I would be getting more help than
this. How can I explain or show you how
bad I am? I have broken bones before,
but the pain was less excruciating
than how I feel inside right now.

It's
okay,
I'm used
to not
being
anyone's
priority, even
my own

How dare I be so upset, unable to
cope, needing support and therapy,
medication, and hating life. what
right do I have to feel this
way? I hate myself
for it.

43

deeply that I had to get this unwell for me to get help.

I had always thought that emotions must be dealt with in private. In secret.

I've been gaslit so many times, its no wonder I got burnt.

The process of healing and therapy is painful and frightening

every day I drag myself out of bed, force a smile, and try to just breathe.

Please ask me how I am. I know you're scared of the answer, but I'm so alone

my heart beat shudders my hollow, exhausted body

In a 'fight or flight' situation I used to be a fighter. I used to be so brave.

I'm hurting.

Being introverted and shy has its perks. I can stay quiet and safe. But it also means I get overlooked as I fade into the background to protect myself. I'm alone, vulnerable, and unable to trust.

Letting someone in, and revealing your emotional turmoil is risky. You become vulnerable to attack or rejection, but it is the only way to show your deepest feelings, and get help.

It devastates me to know there is something wrong with me. I don't know how to make it go away. psychiatric hospital isn't what I had in mind for my 20s. I hate that this is who I have become.

Okay, but where do I find a sense of purpose? A reason to live? A willingness to stay alive? Or is it just an obligation because I was born?

I want a hug

How is it fair that the victim is the one that ends up suffering?

I feel like a lost cause because I don't have the motivation to get better. life terrifies me.

All the people that have treated me like the terrible person I am can't all be wrong.

I'm in such a dark place, and I've lost that small part of me that hoped for more. I want out.

I'm struggling to understand how making me do something that makes me feel worse is in my best interest

I was taught that negative emotions, particularly anger, was bad. so I hid it all away.

I don't feel any more able to cope, there's only so much distress tolerance and journaling I can do. living by constant use of techniques doesn't work

I can't imagine a future that doesn't terrify me

My memory has gone to shit. I can't even remember yesterday. I'm so dissociated. It's scary to have such a bad grasp on reality.

what's so good about life?

I don't get listened to. what I want and need doesn't seem to matter

I'm so grateful for everyone that has helped me

Every breath hurts

There is a difference between not wanting to be alive, and wanting to die. I've crossed that line.

Suicide isn't selfish, oh please god don't say that. think about it. The pain of life has to become so overwhelming, so unbearable, that you want to deny yourself the possibility of getting better just to avoid how bad it is now. To face the unknown of death because it can't be any worse than life. You wouldn't think it was easy or selfish if you felt it. It is the hardest choice to battle every instinct to stay alive, and know you'll upset loved ones. It is a last resort, and NOT easy to think about.

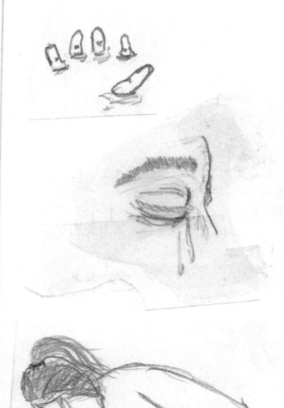

I feel abandoned and left to fend for myself all alone. You know how much I'm struggling, why would you do this to me?

Wishing you were dead from the moment you open your eyes in the morning feels pretty close to rock bottom.

I'm nothing more than a burden. Emotionally, financially, time. I serve no purpose.

46

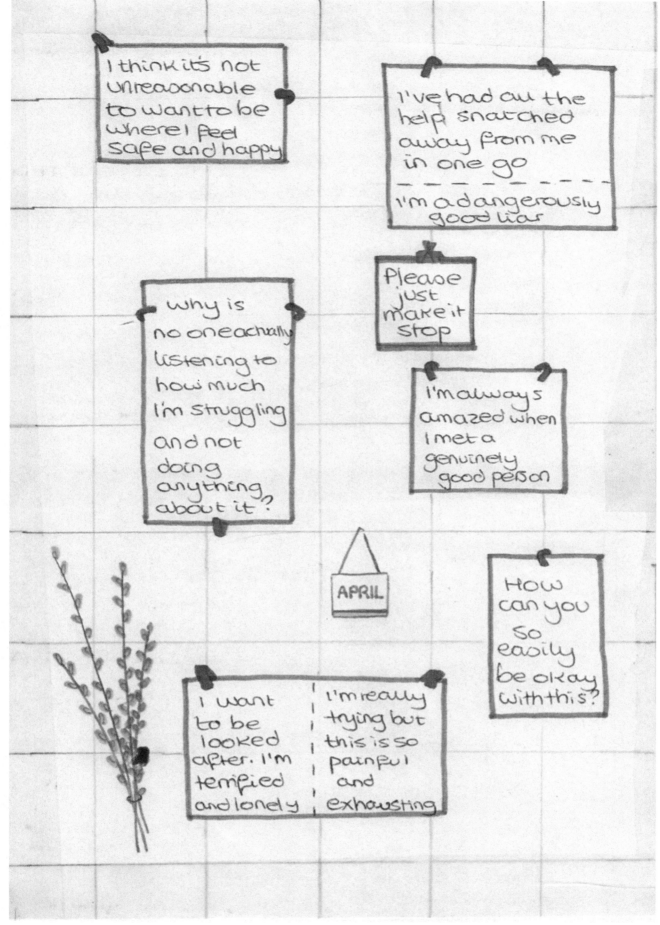

47

my heart and my body aches from all the pain

Please go easy on me, I'm trying my best. Give me time.

How am I always the one that ends up getting hurt, whatever I do?

If you're not going to listen to me, fuck you, but fine. Just don't pretend you are.

I have to want to get better for myself? I'm beyond that point. So now what?

I'm heading for a complete disaster

I'm not feeling anything. If I did it would destroy me

How tragic that being in hospital was the closest to happy I've ever felt.

How can I be expected to live life normally when I can't cope with being alive?

I'm keeping myself so distracted from how I feel, it's exhausting

I'm becoming withdrawn and secretive again. It's all I can do to protect myself.

You're the only one that listens to me and shows they care

All you do is prove my point. Every time.

I'm so disconnected and dissociated that I can't even move sometimes

Every day is getting harder, how can I keep going?

My brain has shut down to protect itself. I can't concentrate, remember or think.

48

'You alone are enough. You have nothing to prove to anybody.'

– Maya Angelou

Using an art medium of your choice, create a piece of art based on themes, associations, actions, etc.
Reflect on the piece and the experience afterwards.

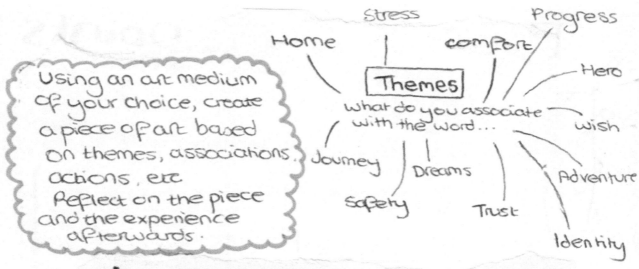

Themes
what do you associate with the word...

Stress
Home
Progress
comfort
Hero
Wish
Journey
Dreams
Adventure
Safety
Trust
Identity

Art therapy

If your current mood was weather, what would it be like?

Activities

draw/create with your eyes closed. what does it look like?

create the masks you "wear"...

create visual representations of emotions. what colours and shapes are they?

Happy
Fear
Sad
Grumpy
calm
excited

I was going to divide these into strengths and weaknesses. But, if recognised and understood, even the "drawbacks" of being highly sensitive can be used in a positive way, as well as properly managed.

Observant

Creative

strongly reacts
to criticism

overthinker

overwhelmed
in crowds

Good imagination

easily overwhelmed

Awareness of
Subtleties

like
alone
time

Good
Listener

Easily hurt

Caring

experiences stimuli of the
5 senses very intensely

Heightened
response
to stimuli

Feeling the
discomfort
or upset
of others

Second guess
their choices
frequently

Soulful

take better care
of others than
themselves

Startled easily

loyal

sensitive
to pain

bottle
up
emotions

Common traits of
a highly Sensitive
person

Intuitive

moved by
the arts

becomes
overwhelmed
easily

dislike
change

will do things
they are not
comfortable
with to avoid
upsetting
others

make others
happy at the
detriment of
themselves

trouble
letting
go

dislike
for
violence

Good instincts
but struggle
to trust them

deep
thinker

unintentional
outbursts of emotion

Put the needs
of others before
their own

Empathetic

take things
personally

conscientious

overly blame
themselves

experiences
emotions
intensely

deeply affected
by the mood
and problems
of others

Strong
conscience

observant

Strong emotional reactions

unlovable

Childish

attention-seeking

Selfish

broken

Weak

crazy

insane

exaggerating

helpless

faking it

Worthless

pathetic

HELLo I AM

Self-involved

Mentally unwell, but I am NOT...

beyond help

A lost cause

Lazy

Lying

manipulative

A liability

untrustworthy

Dangerous

making excuses

Stupid

Aggressive

Wasting your time

"weird"

hopeless

Boring

useless

Violent

— · — Signs: — · —

- low self esteem
- codependency
- fear of abandonment
- putting others first
- need external validation
- fear of the future
- resist change
- shame
- can't tolerate conflict
- trouble asserting boundaries
- people pleasing
- tolerate abuse from others

- crave control
- keep the peace at all costs
- reserved
- untrusting
- feel responsible for others' joy
- reckless impulses
- nightmares
- difficulty forming relationships
- negative world view
- withdrawn
- sleep problem
- self criticism

"Traumatic experiences alter our ability to connect with others authentically. We build walls. We're guided by fear and see "worst case scenarios everywhere. We develop unhealthy coping strategies. Healing makes intimate connections possible again."
—Anna Aslanian

"many trauma survivors hold their breath and their bodies tightly, bracing themselves for whatever is coming next. Staying alert for years takes a toll. create spaces where you can take your armour off." — Dr Thema

— · — Signs you're healing — · —

- Awareness of triggers
- Ask for help
- Able to identify and express feelings and needs
- prevent negative self-talk

- Set and maintain healthy boundaries
- No guilt in having needs
- regularly check in with yourself
- Pride in healing, and acceptance of being a work in progress

Responses

Fight
Anger outbursts
narcissistic
controlling
Agression

Flight
over-thinking
perfectionist
Anxiety
OCD
Avoidance

Freeze
dissociation
difficulty making decisions
isolation
  shame

Symptoms:
- Shame
- domestic violence
- self-sabotage
- insomnia

- irritable
- eating disorders
- nightmares
- panic attacks

Unresolved can look like:
- difficulty trusting
- avoid intimacy
- hard to express emotions

- depression
- victim role
- addiction

In Childhood

'children don't get traumatised because they get hurt; they get traumatised because they're alone with the hurt'
  – Dr Gabor Maté

Impacts:
Not depending on others
Feeling powerless
Easily triggered
Not feeling good enough
Not seeking support

examples:
- Neglect
- Loss of a parent
- Childhood illness
- Poor attachment

- Abuse
- Emotionally unavailable parents
- Serious injury

TRAUMA

Often invalidated

Infertility
Witnessing violence
poverty
Bullying
A loved one with severe illness
chronic pain
loss
oppression
Infidelity
Burnout
unemployment
divorce/ divorced parents

Undiagnosed mental health issues
Abuse
undiagnosed or unsupported learning disability
Addiction issues in the family
Neglect
Racist attacks
Non-consensual sexual experience
Serious injury

Affirmations

- You are not alone, and are worthy of support
- Your experiences and emotions are valid
- It's okay to ask for help
- You have the right to having your trauma validated
- You are not fundamentally flawed
- You are not to blame for childhood experiences
- Your trauma doesn't define you
- You can heal and recover
- You deserve love and connection

On the days when normal tasks feel overwhelming, go easy on yourself and be gentle. Just do what you can.

If you don't feel able to...	Then...
Have a shower	wash your face
Do intense exercise or go to the gym	Go for a walk
Socialise	message or call a close friend
Do the washing up	wash what you need
Brush your teeth, floss, mouthwash	Just brush your teeth
Get dressed up	wear pyjamas or comfortable clothes
Prepare a meal	Order food or make a ready meal
Go outside	open a window for fresh air
Do the laundry or iron	wash one lot of clothes
clean / tidy the house	do one room
concentrate	do easier tasks and take regular breaks
Go to work	Approach the possibility of working from home

Little Wins

- made my bed
- had a shower
- brushed my teeth
- ate healthily
- took the bins out
- went for a walk
- brushed my hair
- did the laundry
- tidied
- cooked a meal
- drank enough water
- walked the dog
- didn't wear pyjamas all day
- did the ironing
- got petrol
- replied to emails
- got enough sleep
- read a book
- did exercise
- went to the shop

Maisie 05.05.07 – 18.06.21

It has been nearly a year since I
lost my best friend, my sister, my
guardian angel. I have always
preferred the company of animals,
but she was more than a dog. Her capacity
for wisdom, logic, and empathy put these abilities in some
humans to shame. She was my sole consistent companion
for 14 years. Verbal communication was one-sided, except
for the odd huff or bark, but her knowing eyes told me she
was listening. I'm convinced she knew what I was saying
to her, or could at least sense my emotions. She understood
me. The love and comfort that radiated from her beautiful
golden coat soothed me and flowed straight to my heart.
She kept all my secrets, her understanding shining out of
her dark eyes. She saw me. She made me feel seen in a way
no one else has. She understood my emotions better than
I do, even now. She responded how she knew I needed her
to; curling up for a cuddle, initiating a game to distract
me, or just sitting quietly with me until the crying stopped.
She protected, guided, and saved me, on multiple occasions.
Her passing has inflicted a pain I can't describe. There is an
emptiness – a sadness in the depth of my heart. She taught
me so much, about life, love, and myself. We grew up
together, aged together, spent her last moments alone, together.
All I have left are the memories, that I will cherish forever.
She has, however, left behind her capacity to love, passing it
on to me and showing me how to love by how much she loved
me. I saw that love is a feeling, not a prize to be
won or lost, it cannot be bought, and doesn't
require verbal communication. It is an instinct.
I will hold on to her memory, to soothe and
comfort my soul. And, honestly, I've fallen
apart without her.

GOOD VIBE LYRICS

'cheer up, baby you're not on your own'
cheer up baby - Inhaler

- - - - - - - - - - -

'I hold your hand and you hold mine. so terrified by nothing'
A Dream Of You - Far Caspian

'I loved you then and i love you now'
Tongue Tied - Grouplove

'I'll never let you go. show me all your flaws, show me your bear claws'
Bear claws - The Academic

'You hold my hand and tell me it's fine. It's getting rough but we're still alive'
Sunlight - Yeno

'don't hide, 'cause we can do anything we want for a while. I think we're gunna be okay. yeah I think we're gonna be okay. These are the days that follow you home. These are the days that kiss you on your broken nose'
These are the days - Inhaler

'Hold on my friend, everything changes in the end'
everything changes in the end - Vistas

'Darling, just hold on. The sun goes down, and it comes back up. The world, it turns, no matter what'
Just hold on - Steve Aoki, Louis Tomlinson

'most my life, I've felt so tired but every now and then when i try, i say keep it up and go on'
KEEP IT UP - Rex Orange County

'You deserve roses on your bedside table'
Balenciaga - New West

'And I'm numb on the outside, but I still feel pain. You better get, you better get, you better get ready for more'
Ready for more - sea girls

'There's tears in my eyes as I am forced to fight against an occupation, one greater than I. So fight on, My little bird. oh, I'm runnin', jumpin', flyin'!
Fight on - The lathums

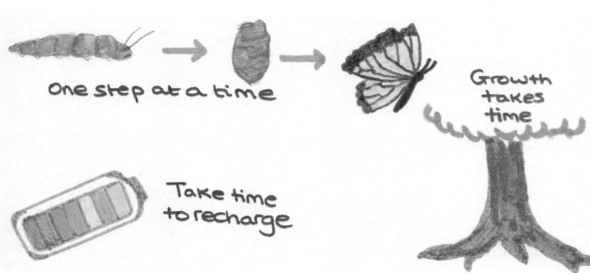

One step at a time

Growth takes time

Take time to recharge

Be Patient

Slow and Steady

GIVE YOURSELF TIME

You are whole. No matter what phase you're in

It's okay if all you did today was survive

You will bloom

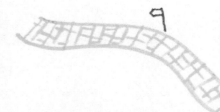

One step at a time

'Keep taking time for yourself until you're you again' - Lalah Delia

Cry. Let the water go. You were drowning.

A sensitive soul with a warrior spirit

Stay away from those that make you feel hard to love

If I'm too much, then go find less

'I hope you understand you need your own love more than they do' - Dhiman

'courage, dear heart' - C.S. Lewis

At first it hurts, then it changes you

tough times make for tougher survivors

learning from mistakes is better than having regrets

'we are made of all those who have built and broken us' - Atticus

There is nothing stronger than a soft soul and gentle heart

What I can control

my attitude

effort levels

Self-motivation

my boundaries

how I respond to situations

my values

what I say

choices I make

productivity

How I treat others

my words

How I treat myself

my sleep

my routine

focus on the positive or the negative

How I behave

How I feel

How I respond to others

My perspective

How I react to challenges

my beliefs

If I forgive

my honesty

How I think

learning from mistakes, or not

If I ask for help

If I help others

How I communicate

If I look after myself

What I can't control

who likes me

predicting

How long a crisis will last

The past

How others speak to me

Other people's motives

The mistakes that other people make

Time

Previous mistakes

The opinion of anyone else

The consequences of others' actions

People's opinions

If others forgive me

What other people do

How others care for themselves

How people respond to me

Other people's feelings

What people think of me

The inevitability of change

certain circumstances

The weather

Beliefs of others

My environment

61

Poetry and quotes

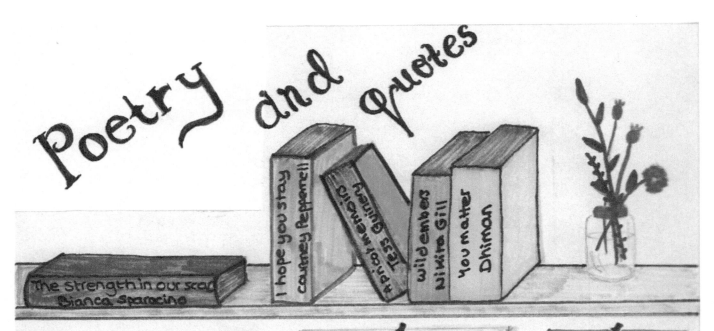

The strength in our scar
Bianca Sparacino

I hope you stay
Courtney Peppernell

Apricot memory
Tess Guinery

Wildember
Nikita Gill

You matter
Dhiman

She carried
the universe
in her mind
and pretended
it didn't hurt

— M.W.P

Darling, you're not
falling apart
you're getting rid
of the pieces
that no longer
serve your purpose.
This is a surgery
of the spirit.
and it can be
painful as hell

— Kalen Dion

And sometimes
that sadness
gets so deep
in your heart
that you
can't even
cry

— Vishal
Rastogi

KEEP TAKING
TIME FOR
YOURSELF
UNTIL YOU'RE
YOU AGAIN

- Lalah Delia

I deserved a better
good bye

- perry poetry

The way they leave
tells you everything

- Rupi Kaur

Scared is what
you're feeling.
Brave is what
you're doing
- Emma Donoghue

Your future
needs you.
Your past
doesn't.

—M.R.

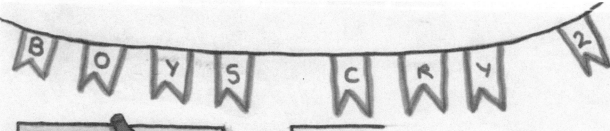

Songs 😞

Numb - Linkin Park

Adam's song - blink-182

All the sad young men - Spector

1-800-273-8255 - Logic

Therapy
crying
Showing emotion
Mental health issues

NORMALISE

Asking for help
Not being okay
Speaking up

Men's mental health

Common Barriers to men Seeking support

* culture, stigma, and gender roles
* resources tend to be female-orientated
* expectation of masculinity
* denial or unaware
* embarrassment
* external invalidation from family/friends
* Access issues
* self medication e.g. alcohol

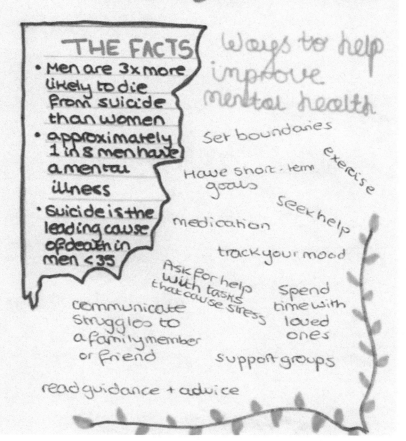

THE FACTS
* Men are 3x more likely to die from suicide than women
* approximately 1 in 8 men have a mental illness
* Suicide is the leading cause of death in men < 35

Ways to help improve mental health

Set boundaries

exercise

Have short-term goals

Seek help

medication

track your mood

Ask for help with tasks that cause stress

communicate struggles to a family member or friend

Spend time with loved ones

support groups

read guidance + advice

 MENTAL HEALTH MYTHS

mental health problems won't affect me

Those with mental health issues are violent and unpredictable

mentally unwell individuals are always unreliable

mental illness can't be cured

mental health challenges occur due to weakness of character and personal flaws

There's nothing I can do to help

overcoming mental illness is just a case of will power

mental health issues can't be prevented

Those with mental health issues can't be high achievers

mental illness can easily be seen in people

only boys have ADHD

mental health issues are the same in everyone

children are too young to have gender identity problems

What I want

- Consistency
- To never feel sad
- To not engage with people or activities
- To cope through the use of negative / unhealthy mechanisms

URGES

HARM

AVOIDANCE

NUMBING

NEGATIVE

'Behind every behaviour there is a feeling. And beneath each feeling a need. And when we meet that need, rather than focus on the behaviour, we begin to deal with the cause, not the symptom.'
– Ashleigh Warner

What I need

- To acknowledge and accept the inevitability of change
- To understand my emotions and experience them with regulation and self-soothing
- To do what I can and not be harsh on myself
- Use tools and skills e.g. distress tolerance or seek help

SUPPORT

MOTIVATION

MINDFUL

SAFETY

COMFORT

INTERVENTION

Secure attachment

Securely attached children may become upset when a caregiver leaves. They respond positively to physical contact, and will usually seek comfort when unsettled.

Dr Gabor Maté

'Anything that is 'wrong' with you began as a survival mechanism in childhood'

Things to say insted of 'Stop crying':

I'm here to listen

I'm with you

Talk to me about it

I understand

I know this is hard for you

Being sad is okay

I know it doesn't feel fair

I will help you

Activities to promote wellbeing

- Set aside time to tackle worries
- Identify 3 good things about the day
- Imagining a positive future
- Talk about feelings

Children's mental health

How to help

- Be patient
- Validate
- Stay calm
- model behaviour.
- Be honest
- Be consistent
- Encourage talking about feelings
- Teach safety
- Relaxation
- Hugs / comfort
- Set boundaries

Kate Middleton

'A child's mental health is just as important as their physical health'

Affirmations

I AM BRAVE   I AM ENOUGH   I CAN DO THIS

MAKING MISTAKES IS OKAY

I CAN MAKE A DIFFERENCE

I DESERVE HAPPINESS

TODAY IS GOING TO BE A GOOD DAY

WHAT A PANIC ATTACK

Nausea

Confusion

Gasping for air

Detatchment from reality

Shaking

Trembling

'I'm dying'

Dizziness

reduced field of vision

Headache

Numbness

Depersonalisation

Heart palpitations

Crying

'I can't breathe'

abdominal pain

Feeling of being chocked

Sweating

Light headed

Blurred vision

Fear of losing control

ringing in ears

Restlessness

muscle tension

Shortness of breath

chills

Racing thoughts or blank mind

Tightness in chest

Feeling of impending danger

Faintness

feeling of unreality or detatchment

Hyperventilating

Unexpected

Selective attention

'I'm going crazy'

Chest pain

Agitation

Intense fear

FEELS LIKE

Our values strongly influence our decisions, behaviour, beliefs, and many other aspects of our lives. Therefore, taking time to identify our own unique combination of values is a vital part of developing a sense of self and helps to motivate us to create a life based on our values, and gain skills to manage situations that don't necessarily align with them. Here are some ideas of potential values:

Perseverance	Understanding	Awareness
Accountability	Openness	Curiosity
Determination	Gratitude	Supportiveness
Trust	Compassion	Respect
Commitment	Honesty	Authenticity
Imagination	Reliability	Purpose
Peace	Forgiveness	Intelligence
Justice		Faith
Stability	Independence	Responsibility
Knowledge	Humour	Kindness
Order	Connection	Community
Freedom	Ambition	Empathy
Adaptability	Leadership	Harmony
Progress	Consistency	Creativity
Wellbeing	Acceptance	Boldness
Courage	Vulnerability	Health
Inclusion	Gentleness	Family
Ethics	Caution	Intuition
Belonging	Loyalty	Wisdom
		Unity
		Calm

Your calm mind
is the ultimate
weapon against
your challenges

mind

tidy / declutter

Bake

Turn off notifications for a while

Read

Create a mood board

Listen to music or relaxing sounds

Learn something new

Focus on self-improvement

body

Nap

Smile

moisturise

exercise

Spa day

have a haircut

create a comfortable space

Rest

Walk in nature

self-care

soul

Yoga

Buy yourself a treat

Scented candle

Cry if you need to

meditate

Avoid the news for a day

deep breathing

create and keep boundaries

Perform an act of kindness

heart

Listen to your favourite music

Reflect on achievements

Make a gratitude list

Unfollow unhelpful social media accounts

spend time with friends or loved ones

spend time in nature

eat your favourite food

4 key types:
- Antidepressants
- Antipsychotics
- Mood stabilisers
- Sleeping pills

Antidepressants
- Used to treat anxiety disorders, depression, phobias, bulimia
- types: SSRIs, SNRIs, tricyclics, MAOIs, other

Antipsychotics
- used to treat: depression, some bipolar types, schizophrenia and personality disorders

Sleeping pills
- benzodiazepine
- non-benzodiazopine
- anti-anxiety or insomnia

Mood
to treat bipolar disorder, mania, hypomania, severe depression

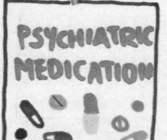

PSYCHIATRIC MEDICATION

Stabilisers
types: lithium, anticonvulsants, antipsychotics,

Often stigmatised, taking a psychiatric medication is not weak or bad

It can help people be stable enough to engage with therapy

Should not be seen as shameful. But an, often, necessary, treatment.

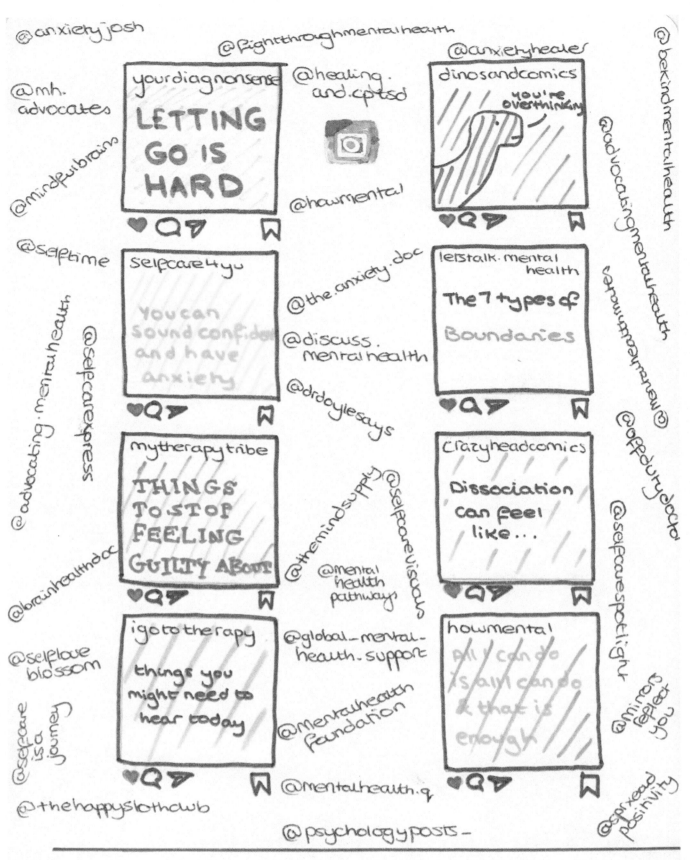

Mental health on *Instagram*

STAY

It may be time to re-evaluate a relationship if ...

Your partner

- Raises their voice in an argument
- Won't make your relationship public
- Is unwilling to apologise for their wrong-doing
- Any abuse
- Demonstrates violence (towards anyone)
- Has a past of being unfaithful or dishonest
- Disrespects your boundaries
- Won't work on themselves or the relationship
- Do not communicate, with no intention of changing this
- Criticises often
- They abuse substances
- Controls your money, who you spend time with, your social media etc.
- Unwilling to recognise opinions different to their own

You

- Minimise yourself to avoid making them feel inferior
- Are the only one putting any effort into the relationship
- Are regularly anxious in their company
- Wait for them to change for you to be happy
- Feel you can't voice your concerns, needs or worries
- Feel judged by them, and so self-doubt a lot
- Feel the need to make excuses for their words or behaviour
- Get more pain from the relationship than happiness
- Feel held back
- Want to keep the relationship for fear of being alone and/or not finding love again
- Don't feel emotionally or physically secure
- Compromise a lot

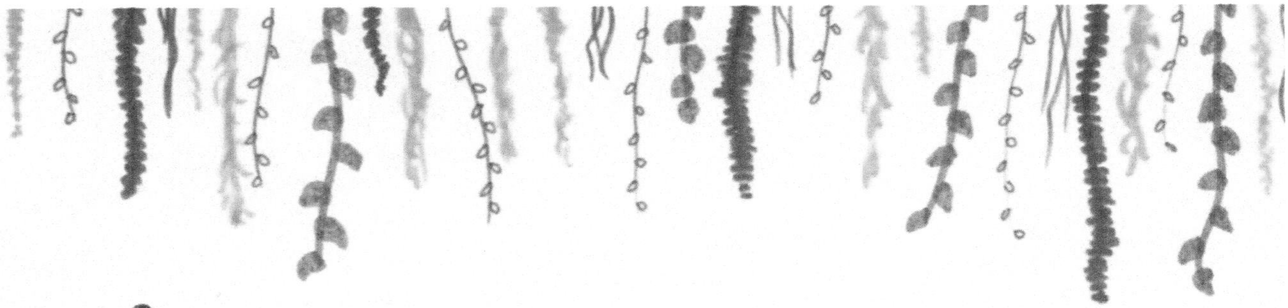

take what you need

Peace

A Chance

Strength

Hope

A break

Courage

Support

Faith

Love

Patience

Forgiveness

Motivation

Wisdom

Reassurance

Belief

Acknowledgement

Luck

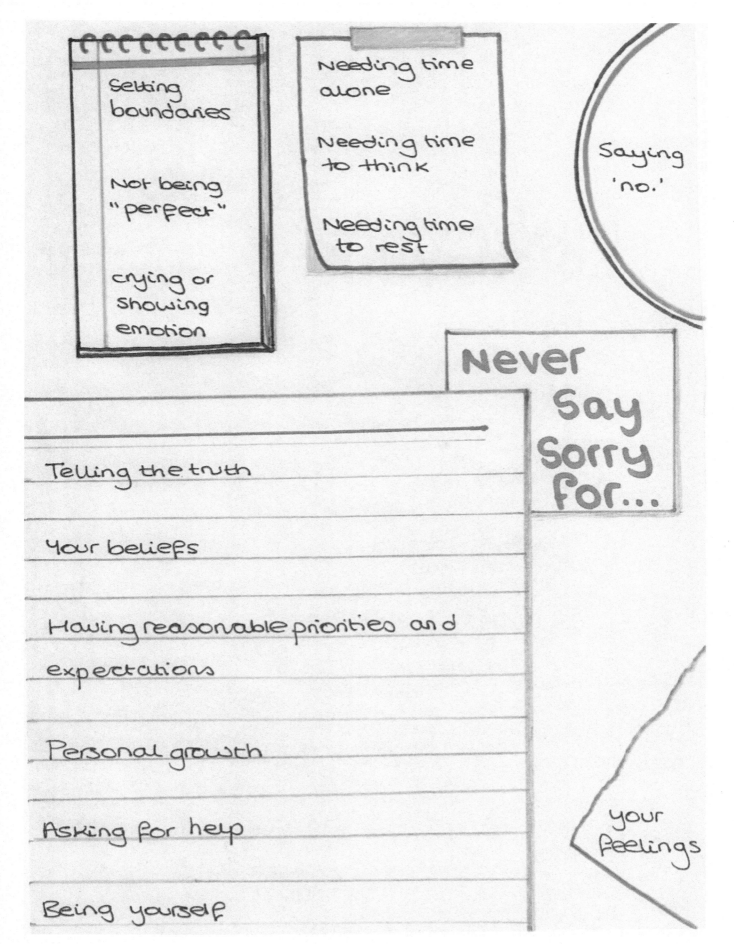

Setting boundaries

Not being "perfect"

crying or showing emotion

Needing time alone

Needing time to think

Needing time to rest

Saying 'no.'

Never Say Sorry for...

Telling the truth

Your beliefs

Having reasonable priorities and expectations

Personal growth

Asking for help

Being yourself

your feelings

IMPROVING

Do not compromise on what is important to you

Focus on what I am able to control or change

Avoid comparing yourself to others

Challenge your inner-critic

Spend time working on yourself such as your values, goals, and boundaries

Reflect on what you are grateful for

Develop a healthy and supportive friend and family network

Identify and work on areas of yourself that you are insecure about

Engage with p or activities make you ho or relaxed

Practice self-care, and remind yourself you deserve it

Journal your achievements and goals

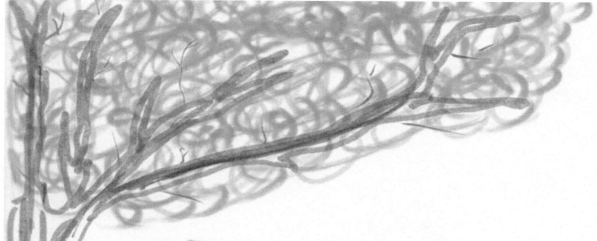

SELF-ESTEEM

Identifying positive affirmations that resonate with you

View failure as lessons and a way to improve resilience

Treat yourself how you treat those you love

Challenge yourself but be gentle with yourself if you make mistakes. Praise yourself for trying.

View your limitations as potential for developing new traits

Remember you are human, and won't be perfect. But that's okay.

Work on internal validation rather than seeking it externally

Stand up for yourself, your beliefs, and your values.

...eople ...hat ...PPY

Exercise. To feel good, not look good

Find meaning and a purpose

Reflect on how far you've come, and everything you've overcome. Remind yourself how strong you are.

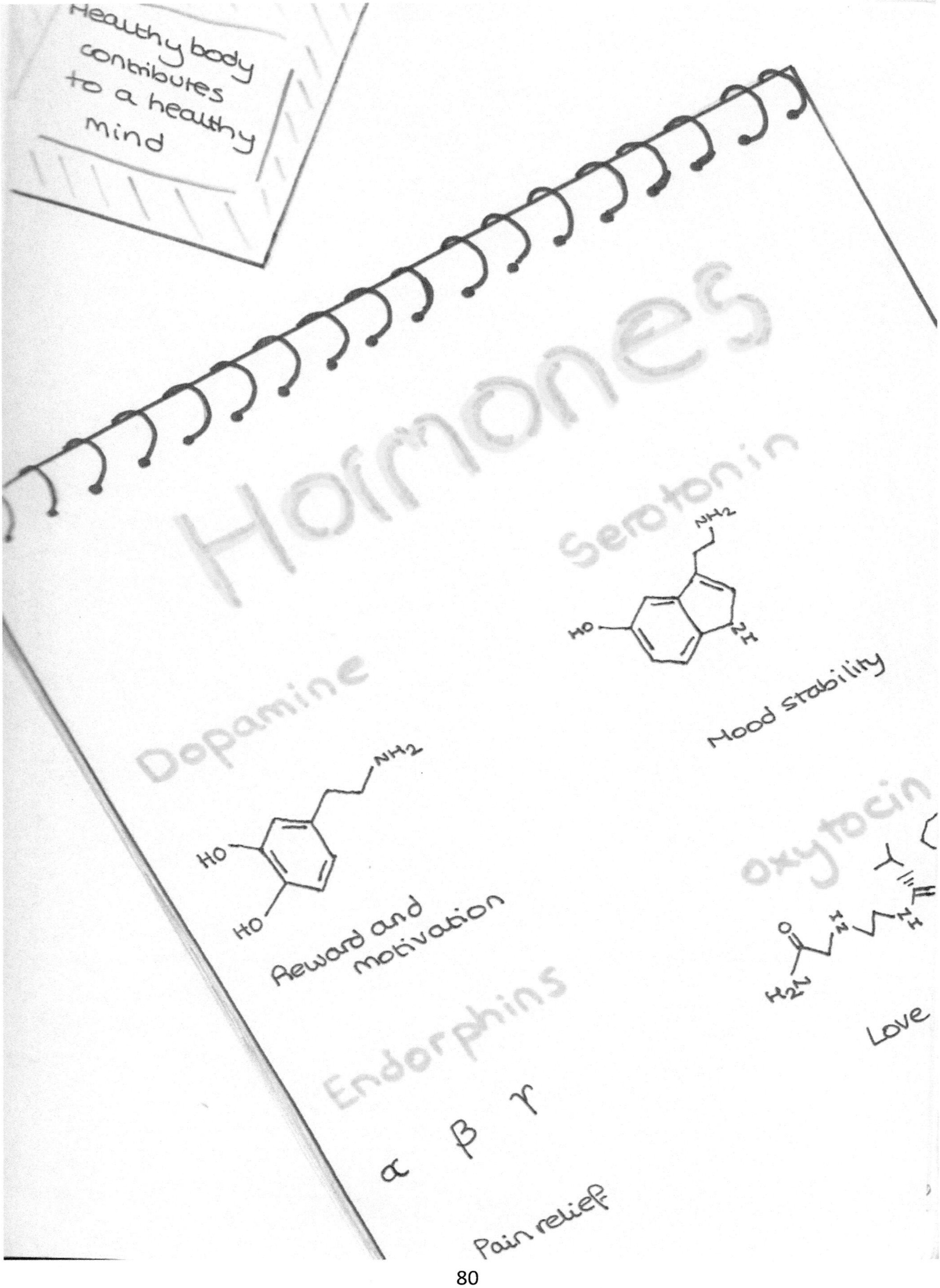

Healthy body contributes to a healthy mind
Hormones
Serotonin
NH_2
HO
NH
Mood stability
Dopamine
NH_2
HO
HO
Reward and motivation
Oxytocin
O
H_2N
NH
NH
Love
Endorphins
α β γ
Pain relief

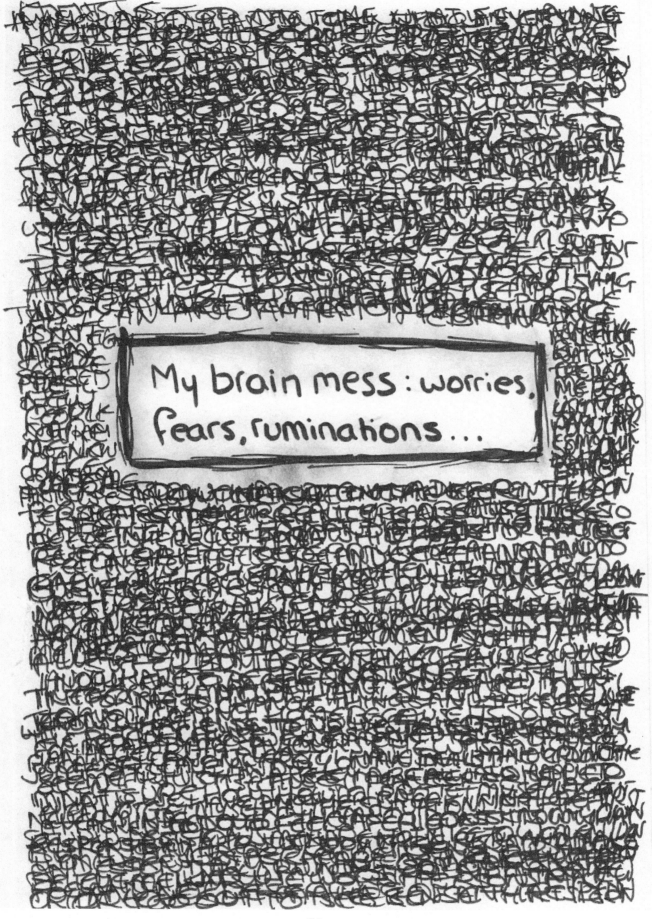

My brain mess: worries, fears, ruminations...

Your emotional struggles are not your fault. But it is your responsibility to heal

No one is perfect, so don't expect it from yourself or others

You can't please everyone all the time

You can't change someone by loving them more

recovery and therapy won't lead to constant progress, there will inevitably be some tough times but fewer

If you hurt someone when you're distressed, you still need to apologise

Hard work doesn't always lead to success

You can't always control your environment

You can't change the past

Not everyone will like you. But that's okay because you don't like everyone

HARD TO SWALLOW PILLS

Some people will not apologise for the damage and hurt they've caused. So you must find closure in acceptance.

Someone who doesn't stand by you at your worst, doesn't deserve you at your best

you can't blame or hide behind your mental illness every time

only you can save yourself

medication isn't a miracle cure. But it can definitely help

Being unwell will effect those around you

You won't succeed every time. But don't lose faith

Ways to help someone who is struggling

- ♡ listen to try to understand, not just respond
- ♡ withold judgement
- ♡ check-in on how they are feeling
- ♡ Prioritise honesty and openness
- ♡ Reassure them that they are enough
- ♡ Remember this isn't their fault
- ♡ Try to tolerate any resistance, it's tough but they are grateful
- ♡ Learn and understand their triggers
- ♡ Set realistic boundaries (time, emotional, physical)
- ♡ Help them to feel safe
- ♡ Get to know how they communicate emotion
- ♡ Be supportive and encourage their progress
- ♡ Be positive, but acknowledge the negative
- ♡ Remind them to challenge their inner critical voice
- ♡ Praise effort, but try not to patronise
- ♡ Be there in difficult moments, your presence is enough
- ♡ Be sympathetic, emotion usually trumps logic
- ♡ Reassure them that they can trust and rely on you
- ♡ Allow them their time to heal

Thank you, just for trying to help

Songs that speak to my Sad Heart

car radio - twenty one pilots

Mercy - Shawn Mendes

Iris - Goo Goo Dolls

Million Reasons - Lady Gaga

Don't Leave - Snakehips

Bad Day - Daniel Powter

Say you won't let go - James Arthur

Oblivion - Bastille

Retrograde - James Blake

Miserable At Best - Mayday Parade

When you love someone - James Tw

The Funeral - Band of Horses

Leave a light on - Yellow card

The Drugs Don't work - The Verve

Tear in my heart - Twenty one pilots

Broken - Jake Bugg

Tonight I wanna cry - Keith Urban

Don't let me down - The chainsmokers

Bitter Pill - Gavin James

Start Again - Conrad Sewell

Unwell - Twenty one Pilots

Heavy - Linkin Park

Last Hope - Paramore

wasting my young years - London Grammar

Everybody Hurts - R.E.M.

Who Am I? - Bazzi

My Blood - Ellie Goulding

Unsteady - X Ambassadors

The End of All Things - Panic! At The Disco

Spiders - Bear's Den

It's not the same anymore - Rex Orange County

Migraine - Twenty One Pilots

Cadillac Dreams - Peter Fenn

Something I need - Ben Haenow

Love me Now - John Legend

Screen - Twenty One Pilots

lowdown - Venbee

Broken Ones - Jaquie

Summer depression - girl in red

Human - Rag 'n' Bone Man

I'm tired of me - Kings Elliot

The less obvious side of illness

Mental illness doesn't just consist of the more obvious and specific symptoms, it also has more subtle indicators and effects that can be easily overlooked. But it is best not to ignore them in yourself or others, as multiple small signs might suggest something is wrong or worsening. Addressing them early could lead to intervention before major symptoms set in. So it is always worth checking in every so often.

emotionally distant

Just waiting for the day to end

overworking beyond your limits to overcome feelings of inadequacy and/or not good enough

feeling empty and numb

Perfectionism and people-pleasing, while neglecting yourself

difficulty showing self-compassion

detaching from emotion

Needing control

accompanying mental health difficulties such as anxiety or addiction

obsessing

seeking external validation

exhaustion

Social isolation

A loss of enjoyment in hobbies

Reduced interest in food, or over-eating

Sleeping too much or too little

difficulty identifying emotions

putting extra effort into "looking better"

talking about struggles, or barely speaking at all

frequent crying

Irritable

Needing to pretend to be "okay"

last minute cancelling of plans

feeling flawed

Negative perspective

needing reassurance and comforting

feeling like a burden

bothered by the "little things"

detachment from reality

85

trigger warning

1:1

A few weeks into my stay in hospital, I was put
onto 1 to 1. This 24 hour monitoring went on for
4 or 5 days, I honestly can't remember as I've
repressed a lot of it. This came about because, on
my 15 minute checks, a staff member came to my
room and saw me pacing, frowning, and chewing
my left thumb nail. She asked what was wrong,
and I hesitantly confessed that I was planning to
use the power cord of the fan in my room as a
ligature. The next thing I knew the fan was gone,
the bedside lamp was gone, my phone charger,
clothes with drawstrings, and shoes with laces. Gone.
Then came the constant observation, even while I
showered, used the bathroom, and slept. I've
never felt more uncomfortable, but also more
protected from myself. I'm naturally a very private
person, so having a member of staff 'arms' length'
away as I slept was very unnerving. I like alone
time to think and unwind, and without this I got stressed
out. I tried to view it as comforting, and a protection
and safety that I couldn't provide myself. But, when
you're suicidal, that's not necessarily what you
want. The loss of independence and privacy weighed
heavy on me, but so did feeling like a burden, that I
was reducing the staff team of someone they
needed. When 1 to 1 ended, I was beyond relieved.

You will find it is necessary to let things go; Simply for the reason that they are HEAVY.

Jane Travis:

'the relationship you have with yourself sets the tone for every other relationship you have'

In order to heal, you need to stop pretending that it doesn't hurt

note to

You are not your thoughts

you are doing your best. Your best doesn't have to be perfect

Focus on you, don't waste energy on the ungrateful

You do not have to prove anything to anyone today

If someone doesn't appreciate you for who you are. You don't have to convince them

Stop saying sorry for :
- Not being perfect
- Showing emotion
- Setting boundaries
- Owning your time

You do not have to do more

You do not have to be more

You are enough, just as you are.

So far, you have survived 100% of your worst days

To heal, you need to stop pretending you're not hurting

do not betray your values and priorities

YOU ARE NOT A BURDEN

Be a bad bitch and a good person. Be both.

It is okay to :
- say 'no'
- ask for help

self

Replacing toxic positivity and invalidation with realistic expectations and validation

Turn this...	Into this...
I'm too sensitive	I'm feeling overwhelmed by this emotion, how can I work through it?
No one cares	People have shown concern in the past. I will try to avoid assumptions
I'm a failure	Is there another way?
Everything is my fault	Think about successes and how I am often capable, and everyone makes mistakes
Nobody likes me	Is this a fair and true thought?
The future is bleak	I am strong enough to face challenges and make changes to improve situations
I can't do anything	I will avoid generalising and I am trying my best
I don't like myself	I can accept my shortcomings as I am only human. I will make an effort to practice self-compassion

MIND GAMES

My mind loves to mess me about and keep me on my toes. I won't know what combination of symptoms I'll have from one day to the next. So, its usually easier to numb everything and feel nothing, just for some consistency.

disproportionate exhaustion
OR
hypervigilance

Insomnia
OR
over-sleeping

Nausea
OR
Hunger

easily distracted
OR
Fixation

Withdrawn
OR
manic

Overthinking
OR
blank

Codependent
OR
isolated

Nervous
OR
indifferent

terrified
OR
risk taking

restless
OR
tired

empty
OR
overwhelmed

extreme emotions
OR
numb

No interest
OR
excessive worry

Helpless
OR
desperate

KARPMAN'S DRAMA TRIANGLE

reliance on others
for problem
solving and
validation

→ feeling... → helpless
→ trapped
↓ → guilty
→ powerless

VICTIM

High dependency

↳ limited ability to make
decisions and assert self

unlikely to
accept blame

PERSECUTOR → quick
to criticise

"helps" others
to improve
self-esteem

RESCUER → selfless

dominating   prioritises   resentful
self over
others

considerate
↳ takes on others'
problems
↳ complaints feel like
failures

The situation can determine the position taken
on the triangle. Individuals can also assume their
position based on beliefs, experience, and personal
traits. Positioning can lead to getting needs met.

Main counselling approaches

- cognitive
- behavioural
- psychodynamic
- humanistic
- person - centred
- Dialectical

you never told anyone

you can't remember all of it

you didn't realise it was traumatic at the time

Your trauma is still valid, even if...

you don't develop PTSD

your life wasn't threatened

others have it "worse"

It happened a long time ago

Social Skills

- accepting differences
- listen actively
- Clear communication
- equal participation
- encouragement
- conflict resolution

Signs of burnout

- Headaches
- self neglect
- Anxiety
- Insomnia
- Irritable
- Physical illness
- Hopeless
- feeling negative

Will this matter tomorrow / next week etc.?

Dispute the truth: is it logical? Useful? real? what else could I think about this?

How likely is it that this worry or fear will happen?

Am I overestimating the risk or danger?

Try not to give emotional or mental attention to unhelpful thoughts

Challenging negative thoughts and catastrophic thinking

How would a friend respond to this?

Mindfully observe the thought for what it is. Allow it to pass.

Are these thoughts helping or hindering me?

Have I dealt with a similar situation that can help in this instance?

Can I put a positive spin on this?

Am I making assumptions?

Am I using 'should' when I don't need to?

Check the facts of the situation

I'm getting so good at
pretending I'm okay

I'm
Broken

'Sometimes,
all you can do
is lie in bed,
and hope to
fall asleep
before you
fall apart'

William C. Hannan

☺   ☺
happy   sad

'Just because
someone carries
it well doesn't mean
it isn't heavy'

Feeling so
much, that
you feel
nothing
at all

Sadness
beyond
tears,
only silence

my heart and
mind are
broken

Small tasks
become
impossible

the bad days

I want to
hide from
the world

Sleep = safe

acting strong
when you've
never felt
weaker

Emotions
OFF

ON

The sadder I am,
the happier I
pretend to be

No interest
or joy.
In anything.

An ache in the
depth of my chest

NOT
ALL
WOUNDS
ARE VISIBLE

'I am lonely
in places I
didn't even know
existed inside me'
Nikita Gill

Isolation

There's so
much I
want to
say but
can't

Journal entries 2022

Some times I'll hear a bark that sounds like Maisie's or a random memory of her comes up. And my heart breaks all over again.

The only thing I like and look forward to is therapy. I can feel what I need to feel and am safe and heard

There's nothing in life that makes all this pain feel worthwhile.

Days that I'm not actively suicidal are "good" days now

It's so frustrating that no one can see how much I'm hurting. It requires me to have some sort of understanding of what's going on, verbalising it, and relying on the other person to listen and try to understand too.

I'm so tense and have pent up emotion that I twitch all the time

It's safer to not interact. I don't need to try and read the conversation and try to convince myself your motives aren't terrible

I'm not able to fend for myself.

Why will no one help me? I'm so scared and alone

I've tried to ask for help in every way I can. I don't even care anymore, so why am I even bothering when its getting me nowhere?

I'm not a priority. I think, in a way, I've always known that.

I've always thought my heart had already broken. But it keeps happening, so maybe its not broken, just slowly falling apart?

What help would I get if I attempted suicide? That's what I need right now.

You keep hurting me, yet won't let me hurt myself.

If you want me alive, please help me feel like its worth while.

Am I being heard and ignored, or am I not making myself heard?

I wish I knew how to explain, and understand, how I feel

The classic move of sitting on the shower floor and hugging my knees as I cry and cry.

That's a go to on the worst of days.

I'm still haunted by that night.

I need help. I don't know how to do this on my own.

I just want to be alone. It's safe, quiet, and easy

I feel worse than I did on one to one in hospital. How doesn't that change anything?

I've had to go back to pretending I'm fine, because if I actually felt how I'm feeling I would fall apart in a big way

I need you to stop gaslighting me. It's making me more confused and feel more insane than I already do.

Do you nor understand how much emotional pain I'm in that cutting my own skin is a way to feel better? It gives me something less painful to focus on

The risk of becoming institutionalised feels like a smaller risk than leaving me all alone

I compromise and sabotage almost every part of myself, just so I don't let anyone down.

I feel like a burden, just by being alive.

What do I want for myself and my life? I don't know. It's never been asked before.

I feel so unwell. I'm hurting, exhausted, aching, overwhelmed, miserable, anxious. And the worst part is having to keep it to myself.

I've tried to keep myself safe, and make my needs heard. I feel like I can no longer be held responsible for what happens to me next.

It's a weird feeling, trying to do the right thing for the wrong reason.

How can I tell you I have everything ready, and I've written my note, and you tell me there's nothing you can do to help me?

I can't bear the pain of life any more

I'm so tired, and I mean a state of complete exhaustion. Even breathing is hard work.

I want to sleep. Just to get a break from my thoughts for a while.

It's so much easier to do things alone

I know what I'm meant to be doing, saying, thinking, feeling. I just can't do it.

I'm not trying to resist treatment, it's just so difficult for me to engage with it

Why am I bothering to protect you? You didn't protect me.

I don't know anything about emotions except how to suppress them change is terrifying. But it can't be worse than it is right now.

It seems to be that the longer you are unwell, the less it matters, and the less people care

I put walls up to protect myself. But now I'm trapped behind them

I'm really good at lying. I even convince myself sometimes

How long do I have to beg for help before self-destruction is okay?

It's easier to just disconnect and feel nothing, even if it means sacrificing any potential happiness

To be fair to depression, it makes you not care about anything so at least you don't get as anxious

Struggling has become my normal

life has pushed me right to the edge. But the step over it is my decision.

I don't have the motivation to do anything good for myself

If I was this close to death with a physical illness or injury I'd have so much more help

If you can't understand, I envy you.

So it would seem that I just don't sleep anymore

99

How sad that therapy and being at the hospital are some of the best parts of my week.

No, I don't look forward to things. I panic about them, I don't want to do them. I feel forced and overwhelmed. But I don't want to ruin anything for anyone else. So, as always, I pretend I'm fine and just go along with it.

I don't feel capable of even half of all the things expected of me. So I feel like even more of a failure, pathetic, and a poor excuse for a person.

One day everyone will wish they'd done more. But now is the time for that.

I want to hurt myself until the world goes silent

I don't expect anything from people, or I expect too much. Either way, it hurts.

I can't keep everything locked up. One day it will all just consume me and I'll be back to where I was before.

I'm so frustratingly useless for the majority of the day. I'm not connecting with my brain so its making me clumsy, not remember things, even struggle to string words into a sentence.

If I leave my emotions unchecked for too long, and they all attack at one, it is completely overwhelming and drowns me. I don't know how to deal with my emotions, so my only effective outlet is to hurt myself. My entirely unhealthy coping mechanism has become a comfort, but it takes over my thoughts and I can't focus on anything else. I watch myself bleed, morbidly satisfied by the growing trickle of red that travels down my arm. Afterwards I sit and think that I must be crazy. That no sane person would want to hurt themselves like this. Most of the time it feels like my mind and body aren't under my control. My survival instincts and common sense scream inside my head, pleading with me to stop. But all I can do is watch my own hands inflict pain on my body. I am not doing this to myself. My body begs me to protect myself. The tiny part of my true self that remains, buried deep within, sides with my instinct, it wants to be saved. But the majority of my soul is out of reach, lost in a deep rooted darkness. This part of me is so dangerous and destructive. It terrifies me.

I waited for someone to notice the grey in my eyes and the emptiness in my smile. It never happened. It took me a long time not only to gather the courage to start the conversation, but to even know how to begin to explain what was going on inside my brain.

One of the worst parts of being ill is that, eventually, you realise that how you are behaving and what you are thinking is utterly fucking ridiculous, childish, and irrational. And yet, you can't stop any of it. There is nothing you can do, you fall victim to your thoughts and the monsters that control your mind. All you can do is watch your sanity disintegrate and your body being slowly destroyed.

The constant pounding head aches, shoulders as hard as bricks, and a stabbing pain in my chest remind me of how much I'm carrying inside me, and helpfully contributing as physical pain.

When I make it back to bed, allowing my fragile mind and exhausted body to collapse, I can release the tears I've held back all day. I'm all alone, I can break down and for once not pretend to be okay. The craving to tear open my skin is stronger than it has been all day. But all I can do is sink into the temporary escape of sleep. This gives me the energy I use to fake a smile, gives life to my heavy limbs, just getting through the day drains me. I wake up tired. I go to sleep tired. I'm in a state of constant emotional and physical fatigue.

I don't trust. It's not what I do. I won't tell you how I'm feeling if I can't be sure how you'll respond. So it's very rare when I actually do open up, so if I do, please be gentle. I'm showing you my most fragile and vulnerable self and she needs validation and to be handled with care.

I've become so good at lying that I'm not even sure how I feel most of the time.

Just because other people don't have to put a conscious effort into staying alive, it doesn't mean I'm not putting everything I have left into it. I don't even want to be alive. This isn't for me.

Do I have a headache from stress, lack of sleep or too much caffiene? I reckon its all 3.

Just because you can't see my pain, doesn't mean its not there.

My body aches with all the emotion its holding

It sucks that for me to have a "good day" I have to feel nothing.

I think I'm a bit scared of getting better. I don't know what its like, and I feel like I'll just go back to being alone again.

I used to think my heart broke years ago, but really I think its just bruised and cracked. Nothing can break this much.

The worse I feel, the more I hide it, so the better people think I am.

I hate that I seem angry. What a horrible way to be thought of.

No one else sees it. So maybe its me?

I know I shouldn't feel abandoned, I know its nothing personal, but I can't help it.

My brain hurts. I'm kinda smart, I'll accept that compliment due to the evidence. But I get too caught up trying to understand the world logically and try to learn new skills and information.

My mind is full of emotions, thoughts and feelings that I have no understanding of. Memories, fears and flashbacks that I'm not sure what they mean. They increase the tension in my head and the pressure-driven headaches, constantly clenching my jaw.

I'm sad no one ever taught me how to use my words to describe how my head and heart are hurting and why. I've tried to show my pain physically but I could break every bone and it still wouldn't be enough.

I want to cry but I can't. I want the release and to let go of all the emotion that's straining my body. But at the same time I've empty and completely void of feeling. I'm numb so I don't get overwhelmed. I pretend to seem how I know I should in the situation. But it's fake.

My body hurts, my limbs ache and are heavy. My chest is so tight that every breath is a laboured effort. My heart beat shudders my hollow body, that trembles with anxiety and fear.

I've lost my spirit, and desire to protect myself. I know how easily I can be overpowered, especially emotionally. And allowing things to happen hurts less than trying to stop them and being ignored. I've tried to "run" from everything but it is constant and exhausted. So I've gone from "fight" to "flight" and finally to "freeze". Where I metaphorically just lay down to die.

In 'fight or flight' situations I used to be a fighter, a brave warrior that could do battle and come off mostly okay. Then one day, my warrior was destroyed.

I'm safe when I'm alone. It's comfortable and what I know. I resented it and called it loneliness for a long time. But I can be who I want and do what I want. No one is there to judge, threaten, expect, or have preconceptions. It took a long time to come to terms with it. So I might as well embrace it. People wonder why I spend so much time alone. It's because its comforting. I like to spend time with people I trust, but this trust takes years to form, and can be destroyed in an instant. It's so fragile and makes me really vulnerable.

I don't know who I am, and that terrifies me. I don't have the energy to find out because I'm always so exhausted just from holding it together and keeping myself alive. People tell me how I should and shouldn't live my life but they're not me and have no idea. But I don't know how to live for myself rather than to please others. I have no sense of self because what I want doesn't tend to matter. I feel like I have to achieve just to have value and to think I'm a good person. But its so draining, because each achievement has to be better than the last.

People call me shy, but its fear. I don't trust anyone and I hate feeling even more vulnerable. I won't initiate an interaction due to fear of rejection or being humiliated. People can judge me, it still hurts, but it won't be anything I haven't already thought about myself.

It's a strange contradiction that part of my mind has given in and accepted what might happen to me, but another part is always on high alert and checking for any potential threat. So despite my fatigued body, my heart beating lethargically, my brain is hypersensitive and won't rest. Just in case. My constant fear of potentially impending physical or mental pain, means I never switch off. My legs won't stay still, shifting my weight, trying not to panic. I breath deeply but its hard work and shaking in my lungs.

Being shy and introverted can have its perks. It's safe and quiet, any drama rarely involves me, and I am able to seamlessly fade into the background. But it does leave me vulnerable, because I struggle to reach out for help. Forming a connection is difficult, mostly its just easier to go it alone. Its what I know. But its when I reach breaking point that this isolation threatens to destroy me. I have to fight every instinct I have just to try and find someone I trust who can help me. But the risk of judgement, invalidation, or disregard is worth it if I find a shoulder to cry on and a heart that cares.

Sleep is so good. Apart from the terrifying, sweat-inducing nightmares. Obviously. I get a break from life, from holding back tears until my head pounds, from thinking, re-thinking, over-thinking. No questions asked, I can escape whenever I want. No pain, no trembling with anxiety, no suffocatingly tight chest, no nauseating stress and fear. nothing. That's all I can do.

Men I don't know or trust are immediately labelled a threat by my cowering mind. I'm terrified of them, as they pose a threat to my safety and body. As a feminist, I hate giving such a suffocating power to strangers. But I know what men can be capable of, even those who say they love me.

I hate myself and I'm furious at myself. How dare I be so depressed and anxious when other people have it so much worse? Particularly when I've made the decisions that made me get hurt. So basically my sadness and vulnerability are all my fault.

I never used to be much of a crier, but now all it takes is for someone to ask me how I am in a sympathetic tone.

- what even is there to live for anymore?
- I'm being held hostage by my own mind
- sleep is great. life stops, but you don't let anyone down.
- How can you still believe me when I say 'I'm fine' when there are tears in my eyes and scars on my body?
- why is there never anyone or anything I can rely on?
- How do I even begin to explain my demons to you when I don't understand them?
- I need to learn how to release my pain through words, either written or spoken. Rather than through blood, scars, and tears
- I got lost in this darkness, and now i can't find myself again
- Sleep saves me. I can be alone but not lonely. I can leave life with no guilt. I can be who I am.
- my mask is starting to break
- was there ever a time when I didn't want to end it all? I don't remember

by others...

- humiliate
- trivialise
- accuse
- taunt
- threaten

isolate from friends and family

make you feel sorry for them and put you down

silent treatment and manipulate

control your behaviour

- lack of respect
- belittle achievements and goals
- jealousy

gaslight, blame, passive aggression

Emotional abuse

- self criticism
  - ↳ too...
  - ↳ should...
  - ↳ not...
  - ↳ can't...

self-sabotage:

unrealistic expectations

overdoing it or carrying on

- overindulgence with disregard of consequences
- perfectionism

making comparisons with others (particularly your worst to their best)

not resting, "powering through" burnout and not saying 'no' to requests

ignoring your needs, numbing emotions, denial, avoidance

holding back from opportunities e.g. don't feel worthy

# of self...

procrastination to a point of high stress

BE

KIND

TO

YOUR

MIND

 ways to view life:
1. No one cares 🙁
2. No one cares! 🙂

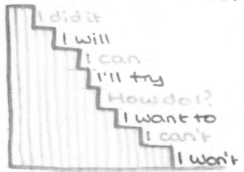

I did it
I will
I can
I'll try
How do I?
I want to
I can't
I won't

Steps to overcoming mental illness

Not ENOUGH — FEAR — Too MUCH

The fear of not being enough, and the fear of being too much are the same. They're the fear of being you.

Without its ups and downs, there would be no life.

FIGURES

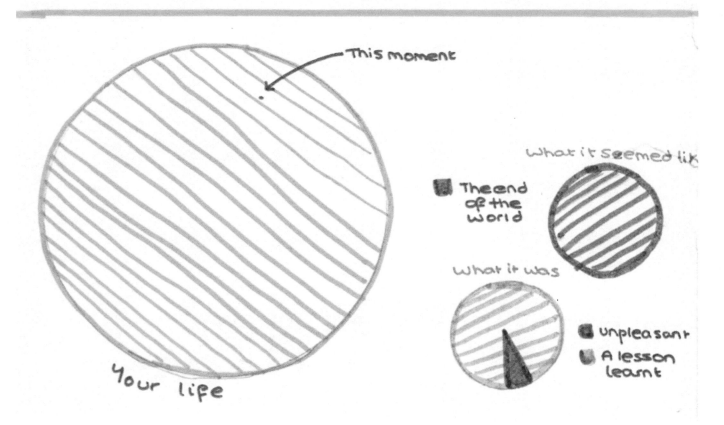

This moment

Your life

What it seemed like
■ The end of the world

What it was
■ unpleasant
■ A lesson learnt

RESILIENCE

Resilience comes from practicing and developing a mindset that helps to cope with and overcome setbacks such as rejection, loss, or heartbreak

"you may not control all the events that happen to you, but you can decide not to be reduced by them"

Maya Angelou

Negative experiences are sadly inevitable. But the choices we make in response can change

Traits

- Self control
- optimistic thinking patterns
- seek assistance
- recognise emotions
- learn from mistakes
- willingness to overcome difficulties
- accept weaknesses
- self esteem
- healthy coping mechanisms

optimism → flexibility

ability to problem solve

focus on action

self belief and confidence

emotional awareness

light hearted response to setbacks

good communication

network of support

self control

ability to respond to circumstances

Developing resilience:

embrace change

work to understand yourself better

Practice identifying what you are grateful for

recognise or create a lesson learnt

DAILY ROUTINE

Based on energy levels:

NO ENERGY

Be kind to yourself

Give yourself permission to rest

Do or watch something comforting

Try to resist external pressure to do too much

Take time to reflect

LOW ENERGY

Do some easy housework

Do some light exercise or walking

Spend time outside

Speak to a loved one

Plan tasks for days with more energy

MID LEVEL ENERGY

Get work done

do more tasking chores and jobs

learn something new

prepare meals for low energy days

do some more intense exercise

Suicide. My perspective.

Please bear in mind, I am in no way advocating suicide, and remember I am still unwell. I know my opinion and perspective is skewed, but it feels like it needs to be said.

Suicide is not easy, selfish, a cop out, or however else you want to judge it. I have been repeatedly blackmailed into staying alive and it hurts so much. I would ask these people to consider how much distress and pain a person has to be in to want to deny themselves a future, deny themselves the chance of recovery, to face the unknown of death because it can't be worse than the pain of life. It is a terrifying thought and contradicts every survival instinct, so isn't "easy", if anything it is hard, but when it becomes an attractive option, it is usually the last possible option.

Personally, I've tried and tried to save myself. Sometimes I can, other times I can't and I need someone there to help me. It's not something you do when things get a little tough. It's when the hellish weight of life and constant distress are too overwhelming to endure. I don't think anyone wants to die, they just desperately can't see any other way out, that their suffering is so intense that it seems it will never cease.

If you can't relate to feeling suicidal, and I hope you can't, please just remember to be kind and to avoid judgement. The guilt I feel every time I want to take my life is enmeshed with a self-hatred about the pain I would cause. Having been told the distress I would cause, I not only feel ashamed but also invalidated. It seems that to stop others from suffering I must prolong my own. What about preventing my pain? Why won't anyone do that? We go full cycle back to the self-criticism and feelings of worthlessness that got me to this place to begin with. So, overwhelmed by agony, I retreat back to my withdrawn silence and pretence. It hurts the same, but I don't get judged this way.

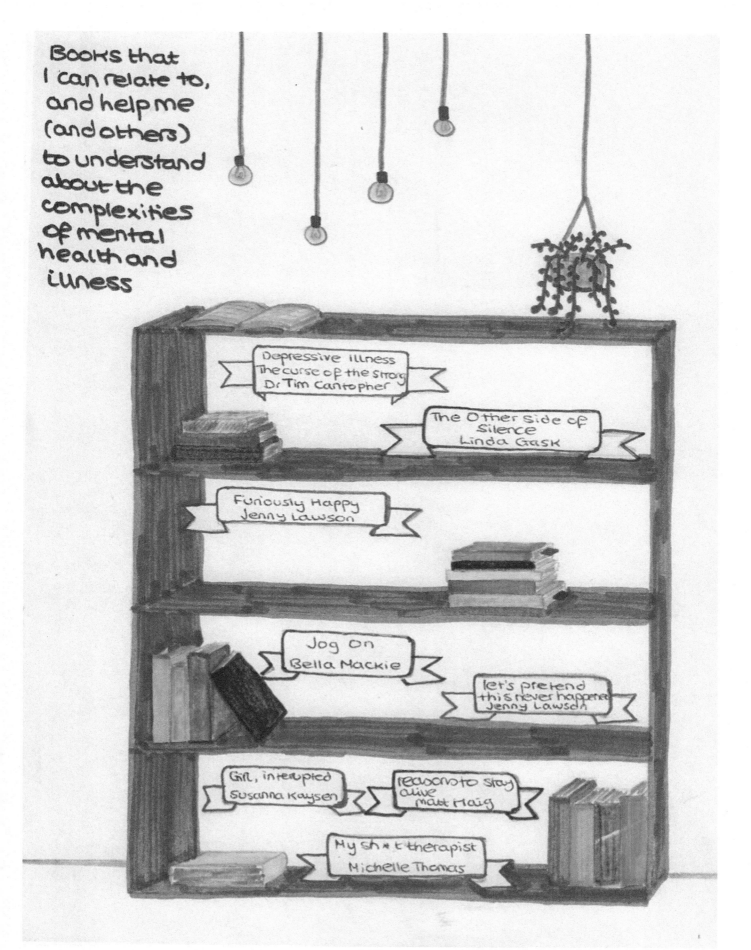

Books that I can relate to, and help me (and others) to understand about the complexities of mental health and illness

Depressive illness
The curse of the strong
Dr Tim Cantopher

The Other Side of Silence
Linda Gask

Furiously Happy
Jenny Lawson

Jog On
Bella Mackie

Let's pretend this never happened
Jenny Lawson

Girl, interrupted
Susanna Kaysen

Reasons to stay alive
Matt Haig

My sh*t therapist
Michelle Thomas

Don't wait until
you reach your goal
to be proud of
yourself.
Be proud every
step you
take.

- Karen Salmansohn

How have you been Sleeping?

What are you looking forward to?

What did you do today?

What made you smile recently?

It's good to see you how are you?

What could we do together?

What's on your mind?

What's your vibe today?

What topics are off the table for today?

Is there anything you want to talk about?

What do you need?

What do you listen to at the moment?

What emotion are you feeling?

Ways to check in with others...

I'm so glad to see you

What are you grateful for right now?

I have read up on... so I can help

What are your main 3 feelings today?

How could I help you?

Is there anything you want to get off your chest?

how did that make you feel?

What nice thing have you done for yourself recently?

do you need some space?

What can I do to support you?

thank you for trusting me, can I support you somehow?

I'm happy to listen

do you feel like talking?

What is your focus for today?

A Letter to my younger self

In the darkest depths of mental and emotional distress, self compassion can seem unattainable. Instead, it can be easier to direct care and sympathy to another. Writing to a friend, or your younger self, in a compassionate tone can be a helpful way to begin to direct this kindness towards yourself. When writing to your younger self, it also helps to nurture your inner child and start to face the past in a constructive way.

Dear young me,

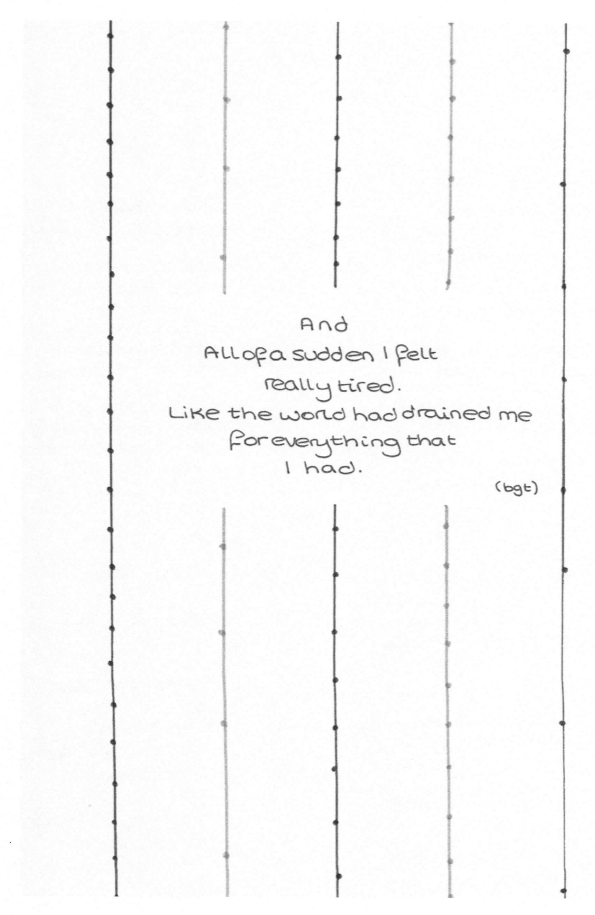

And
All of a sudden I felt
really tired.
Like the world had drained me
for everything that
I had.

(bgt)

STRESS VS. ANXIETY

Short term	longer term
response to trigger ↳ external origin	may not have an identifiable trigger ↳ internal origin
feeling overwhelmed	feeling worried and fearful
can lead to burnout	can lead to a panic attack and/or an anxiety disorder
manageable with coping strategies	manageable with coping mechanisms, therapy and/or medication
occurs in most people at varying intensities	

SADNESS VS. DEPRESSION

Short term	long term
normal and natural experience of emotion	mental health issue
upset	low mood
can maintain productivity, and other abilities	lack energy, motivation, memory, concentration
still feel like yourself	changes in thoughts, behaviours, idea of 'self'
can be overcome with time and/or coping mechanisms	requires medical help

Self-reflection prompts

- What would you forgive yourself for?
- What does unconditional love look like to you?
- How do you set and reinforce boundaries?
- What does your authentic self look like?
- What would you say to someone who has betrayed you?
- What is a trait you see in others that you wish you had?
- What were your parents' values, and how did they influence yours?
- When are you hardest on yourself? Where do you think this comes from?
- What is most important to you?
- What are the first signs that your mental health is declining?
- Think of a time you were wronged as a child, how has it impacted you?
- Who does your inner critic sound like?
- Which of your current relationships needs healing?

What does happiness feel like?

What are you most afraid of?

What do you need to feel safe?

What in your life needs to change for you to heal?

What do your daily habits say about you?

What is preventing my happiness?

How can you tell what someone else is feeling?

What makes you feel proud?

How will you be able to accept things you won't get an apology for?

Questions to an

What do you value most about yourself?

Where do your insecurities come from?

How would you describe yourself positively?

When do you feel useful to others?

What purpose do you want for yourself?

How can you forgive and move on?

What does your authentic self look like?

What can you do today to make tomorrow a little better?

Why do you compromise yourself to please others?

What support do you need?

What makes you feel a bit better?

What would you like from life?

How are you feeling?

How do you reinforce your boundaries?

Why do you feel sad?

What are you most afraid of?

What inspires you to survive?

How could you be kind to yourself?

I Struggle

How does (insert emotion) feel in your body?

swer

What are you most worried about?

What do you like about yourself?

What do you do to care for yourself?

What does your future look like?

What is your biggest priority?

What helps you to cope that is a healthy choice?

What good qualities do you have?

When do you feel confident?

RECOVERY

Healing is a process. It can feel like it is...

lonely   daunting   sudden   slow   boring

Hopeful   upsetting   complicated   scary

hard work   motivating   messy   overwhelming

invigorating   a relief   progress   changeable   inspiring

The harsh truth:

It isn't a linear process. It will take time. But your health and wellbeing deserve to not be rushed. Trust yourself. Devote yourself to yourself.

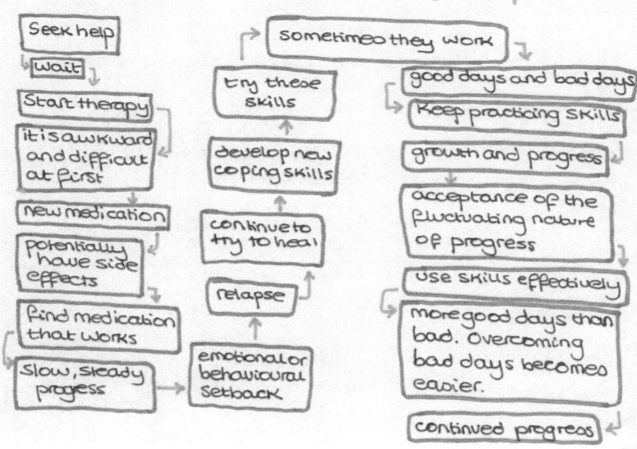

- Seek help
- Wait
- Start therapy
- it is awkward and difficult at first
- New medication
- potentially have side effects
- find medication that works
- Slow, steady progress

- Sometimes they work
- try these skills
- develop new coping skills
- continue to try to heal
- relapse
- emotional or behavioural setback

- good days and bad days
- Keep practicing skills
- growth and progress
- acceptance of the fluctuating nature of progress
- use skills effectively
- more good days than bad. Overcoming bad days becomes easier.
- continued progress

FLOWERS

Grow back
Even after
The harshest winters
You will too

— Jennae Cecelia

The brain

Forebrain

receives and processes sensory information, controls endocrine function, and reasoning

Hind brain

spinal cord + cerebellum. The latter controls movement and balance

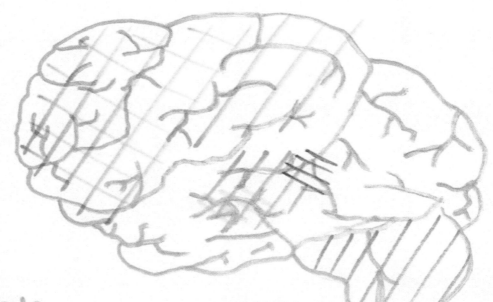

Midbrain

motor movement, audio-visual processing, the temporal lobe is responsible for emotions and memory

A more active amygdala, which initiates survival responses

Reduced hippocampus volume, leading to memory issues ←

Impacts of trauma

PTSD can lead to a reduced volume of the prefrontal cortex, impacting rational thinking and emotion regulation

126

'I'm sorry I haven't been myself and something's got me down. What it is I cannot tell'

-Freakin' out on the interstate - Briston Maroney

'Am I the only one I know waging my wars behind my face and above my throat?'
- Migraine
- Twenty One Pilots

'Tell me that it's all okay'
- Stay - Post Malone

'People wonder if I'm fine. Well I'm finding that question hard to answer. Coming up empty inside'
- L-Train - Toledo

'Holding on to so much more than I can carry. I keep dragging around what's bringing me down. If I just let go I'd be set free'
- Heavy - Linkin Park

'You know I've been fucked up, crazy. It's been a little heavy lately'
- It's been a little heavy lately - Joesef

'Can you hear me? S.O.S. Help me put my mind to rest'
-S.O.S - Avicii

'I'm not crazy, I'm just a little unwell. I know, right now you can't tell'
- unwell
- matchbox twenty

'Sad face girl in a mixed up messed up fucked up world'
- Sad Face baby
- The Lathums

Lyrics that say it better than I can

⏮ ▶ ⏭

'I'm so tired of being paper thin, like I could tear at any time. Trapped inside of the brain I'm in, please get me out of my mind'

- Who Am I?

- Bazzi

'Feeling numb where we belong. Afraid to see what we've become'
- Movie in my mind
- Saint Raymond

'Hold on to me 'cause I'm a little unsteady'
- Unsteady
- X Ambassadors

'You know, I'm terrified that maybe I wasn't cut out for this. You know, you could come and save me'
- terrified
- isaac gracie

'It's almost like you're screaming but no one hears your voice. 'Cause everything is changing. You find your way but it's never enough'
- New Normal
- Khalid

'I think I'm dying 'cause this can't be living'
- Maybe you're the reason - The Japanese House

'I don't wanna be alive I just wanna die and let me tell you why'
- 1-800-273-8255 - logic

'It's not that rare for me to let myself down'
- It's not the same anymore - Rex Orange County

'One thing I like about me is that I'm nothing like you'
- MEAN!
- Madeline The Person

127

Sometimes,
it is best to just let
things go

emotional intimacy

- Safe environment to be vulnerable
- feeling seen / heard
- feeling ease in their presence
- accountability and respect
- can freely express emotions
- meaningful conversation
- able to share insecurities
- supportive of dreams and individuality
- shared experiences

Codependence

- unhealthy reliance on another person
- people-pleasing behaviour
- unrealistic expectations
- seek external validation
- lack independence
- can be replaced with healthy interdependence
- blurring of boundaries
- can be a response to trauma
- feel responsible for the other

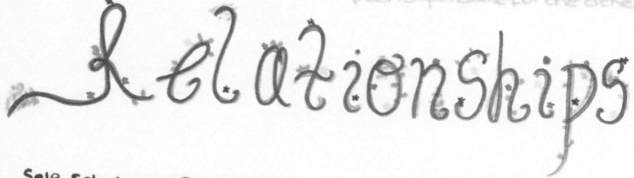

Self Sabotage of relationships

- expect rejection and/or pain
- not feeling worthy of love
- repeating the past
- making false assumptions
- ending relationships for fear of being abandoned so keep control
- lack of trust
- extreme selflessness to keep the relationship stable
- cause pain to fulfil predictions
- cyclic suffering
- requires addressing to avoid the same pattern

respect

- Taking responsibility
- Acknowledge and show compassion
- listen attentively
- supportive of goals
- Timely apologies
- Avoid hurtful humour or comments
- Keeping confidentialit
- pride in your partner
- healthy boundaries and independence
- communicate concerns
- Trust

POSITIVES

'Walls keep everybody out. Boundaries teach people where the door is' - Mark Groves

↳ encouraging openness, respectful communication, and establishing agreed boundaries helps build and maintain healthy relationships

↳ A general awareness and practice of these skills, or therapy, can positively impact relationships

Learning to express emotions through healthy coping mechanisms and communicating fears or needs

↳ allows support within the relationship

↳ encouraged in a therapy setting, making it easier to apply to wider environments

↳ sharing thoughts and feelings brings closeness

Improving self-esteem and confidence can result in relationships based on mutual respect and healthy independence and interdependence

THE IMPACT ON RELATIONSHPS...

Trauma, or unpleasant experiences, can lead to self-sabotage in relationships due to an expectation and fear of pain and the past repeating itself

Poorly developed ability to be emotionally close and vulnerable within the relationship can cause distance

Discomfort with emotional and/or physical intimacy

Feeling unworthy or undeserving of love can cause people to push loved ones away

Low confidence, trust issues, and poor self-esteem can lead to the need for continual reassurance of the relationship

NEGATIVES

Education, and learning from those who have experienced illness

Reducing

mental

Encouraging conversations about emotional wellbeing, and offering support

illness

Avoiding the use of negative terms, and checking the facts so as to make assumptions

Show respect, understand that the person is not their illness, prioritising equality

Stigma

TIP OF THE
ICEBERG

ANXIETY

anger over planning
on edge
avoidance insomnia

depressed jealous
rejected
overwhelmed
guilty grieving
regretful hurt
lost
stressed blamed
embarrassed
shame
helpless

ANGER

insecure nervous
sad violated
jealous rejected
embarrassed
shame
anxious
vulnerable

Coping Skills

Regulate and Self-soothe using your 5 senses

Distract yourself (but don't avoid)

Try not to reject reality

Radical acceptance

Of the present moment and yourself
Mindfulness

Direct your awareness towards the emotion and allow it to come and then go while simply observing it

use your 5 senses

Deep breathing

Meditations

Gratitude

Practice self-compassion

Just notice

Journaling
thoughts   values
Goals

TIP
temperature e.g. hold ice

progressive muscle relaxation

Intense exercise

Do the opposite action e.g. read or write positive affirmations

positive self-talk

Exercise

Speak to someone e.g. a friend or therapist

colour   Write   paint
Be creative
Poetry   draw

Read

listen to calming music or sounds

Yoga

Spend time with loved ones

Take a bath

prioritise and organise

Forgive

Hug someone a pet, or a stuffed toy

Get enough sleep

Watch a favourite movie or TV show

use a stress or fidget toy

emotion

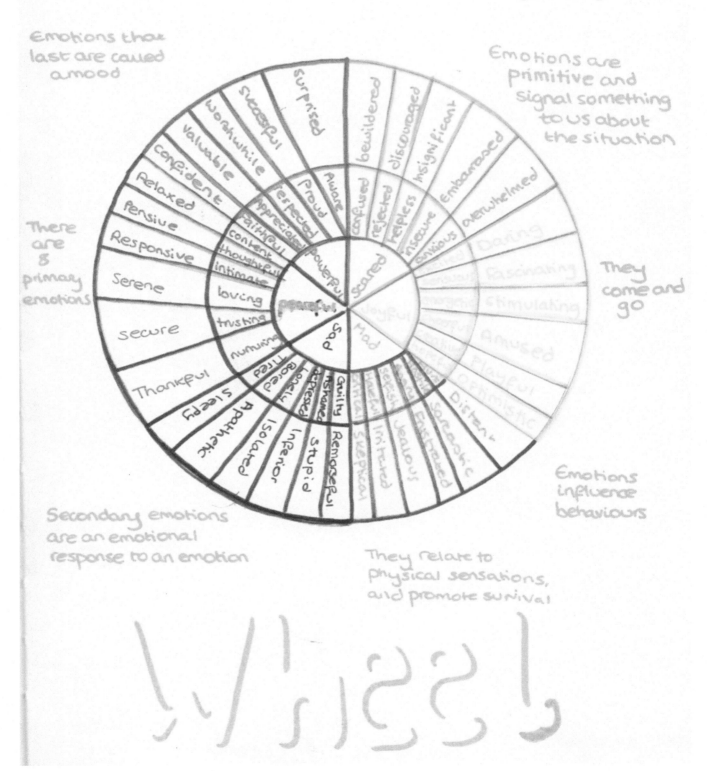

Emotions that last are called a mood

Emotions are Primitive and Signal something to us about the situation

There are 8 primary emotions

They come and go

Secondary emotions are an emotional response to an emotion

Emotions influence behaviours

They relate to physical sensations, and promote survival

Wheel

Emotion wheel labels

Surprised, Successful, Worthwhile, Valuable, Confident, Relaxed, Pensive, Responsive, Serene, Secure, Thankful, Sleepy, Apathetic, Isolated, Inferior, Stupid, Remorseful, Guilty, Jealous, Distant, Optimistic, Playful, Amused, Stimulating, Fascinating, Daring, Overwhelmed, Embarrassed, Insignificant, Discouraged, Bewildered

Aware, Proud, Appreciated, Faithful, content, thoughtful, intimate, loving, trusting

Powerful, Scared, Sad, Mad, Joyful, confused, rejected, helpless, insecure, envious

Peaceful

Tired, Bored, Lonely, depressed, Ashamed, hateful, Injured, selfish, Sorsaoke, Enchanted

'you are so
brave and
quiet,

I forget you are
suffering'

— Ernest Hemingway

Reasons To Consider Therapy

emotions

Kind words

Safe space

non-judgemental

comfort

listened to

thoughts

Validation

reliable

without guilt

feelings

where appropriate

no shame

focus on you

healthily/ appropriate

YOU DESERVE HELP IF YOU NEED OR WANT IT

Saying things aloud

to understand

insight

To someone impartial

techniques

ways to cope

support

professional input

advice

To make progress

challenge

Suggestions

negative thoughts

consider other perspectives

beliefs about self, others, etc.

destructive coping mechanisms and behaviours

feedback

136

Trigger warning

Not just here, not just when its a possibility, and not just in painful hind-sight. Prevention is by far better than cure, especially as a cure is unlikely once an individual has reached that level of distress. Recovery is possible, but shouldn't be a factor, it would be so much better to help people before the requirement to heal. Support, comfort, listening, and awareness of warning signs are better than regret, grief, remorse, and loss.

We need to talk about suicide

Warning signs	Risk factors	Prevention
• behaviour changes (sleep, eating, etc.)	• Bullying	• learn warning signs
• self harm	• Unemployment	• Listen
• extreme mood swings	• Loss	• speak up
• loss of interest	• Relationship issues	• encourage seeking help
• expressing hopelessness	• Homelessness	• keep in contact
• Giving away items	• Financial issues	• minimise their time alone
• Talking about death	• Mental illness	• distract
• Social withdrawal		
• Saying goodbye	• Substance abuse	• emotional support
	• Abuse	• Reach out
• Thinking of themself as a burden	• Trauma	• Ask what they need
• excessive crying	• Lack of support	• find resources

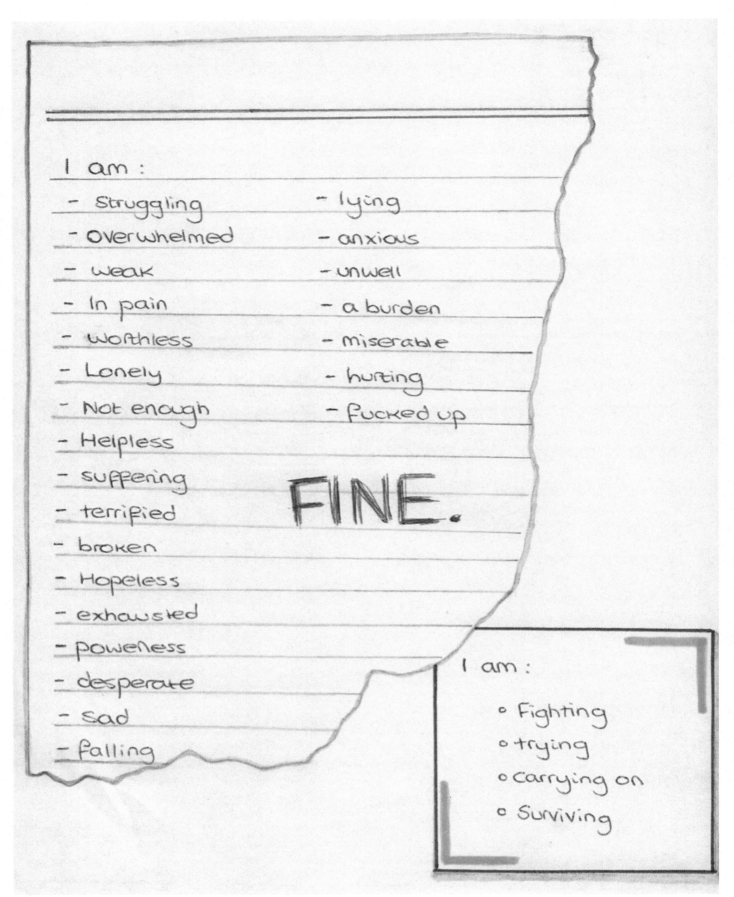

I am :
- Struggling
- Overwhelmed
- weak
- In pain
- worthless
- Lonely
- Not enough
- Helpless
- suffering
- terrified
- broken
- Hopeless
- exhausted
- powerless
- desperate
- sad
- falling

- lying
- anxious
- unwell
- a burden
- miserable
- hurting
- fucked up

FINE.

I am :
○ Fighting
○ trying
○ carrying on
○ Surviving

For yourself

Budgeting

Setting aside time for exercise

Time restrictions
→ Bedtime
→ wake up time
→ time used for work/leisure

diet and food
→ health value → consumption
→ Meals out
↓
Food shopping

Avoiding Procrastination

Regular healthcare
↓
dentist
→ doctor

limiting alcohol intake

Not taking on other people's issues

when appropriate ← as my responsibility to resolve → especially if I feel overwhelmed with my own challenges

Personal hygiene

Saying no if my morals, safety, or beliefs are violated

Asking for help

Not neglecting yourself to please others

Boundaries

A form of self-care and respect

Saying 'no'

not taking responsibility to fix others

Nothing against the other person, but instead it is for you

Expressing needs

Awareness of each other's independence

The right to safely express discomfort

Not prioritising one party over the other

How much time is invested in the relationship

boundaries have been mutually agreed

proximity, personal space, and sexual closeness are mutually agreed and respected

maintaining personal boundaries and an awareness of unique needs and values

peace, safety, and compassion

respect the need for privacy

everyone is entitled to their opinion

Balance, acceptance and understanding

No resentment

With others

139

Habits that can improve mental health

Physical
- 7 to 9 hours of sleep
- regular exercise
- hydration
- balanced diet
- Hygiene
- physical closeness
- Sunshine or vitamin D
- deep breathing
- resting

Mental
- meditation
- gratitude
- emotional connection
- limit social media use
- trying new things
- hobbies / exercise
- reading
- socialising
- affirmations

Routine
- wake up time / morning
- dental and medical
- cleaning and tidying
- meal planning
- Skin care
- laundry
- evening wind down
- regular social interactions
- time for self-reflection

Psychological
- goal setting
- challenging negative thoughts
- talking about troubles
- stress and workload management
- supporting others
- recognising achievements
- mindfulness
- support network
- develop problem solving skills

--Not so helpful things to say to someone --
--with depression--

cheer up

We all have bad days

Chin up, things could be so much worse

How can you be depressed when you have/are ___?

Oh, yeah, I get so depressed too sometimes.

Oh my god I was so embarrassed I wanted to kill myself !!

What do you have to cry about?

↳ when said as a joke. But do NOT dismiss it as a passing comment if in any doubt. Be safe, not sorry.

There's so many more people that have it worse than you

Grow up

Get a grip

You're too sensitive

I had a bad day last week, so I totally get it

But, you don't look depressed!

Have you tried just smiling and carrying on?

you're so emotional

you're probably just tired

Talking about it won't make it any better. Try not to think about it.

I don't believe in popping pills, it messes you up.

Therapy is very self-indulgent

Is it hormones?

But it's your mind, can't you just choose to be happy?

Suicide is selfish, weak, the easy option

you're mental

Get some fresh air, you'll be fine

FOUR WORDS

[I'm losing my mind] [every day gets harder] [waking up is painful] [I do everything wrong]

[This is my fault] [My heart is broken] [This needs to stop] [You're paid to listen]

[I'm hurting too much] [People will hurt me] [I can't do this]

[I'm out of control] [Nobody cares about me] [I'm broken and helpless] [Why should anyone care?]

[Life isn't worth this] [Nothing is really helping] [I don't understand life]

[I can't go on] [You really scare me] [emotions don't make sense] [my pain is constant] [I won't open up]

[This hurts too much] [I'm powerless and weak] [I am so pathetic] [I disappoint my family]

[I'm really not enough] [I'm only getting worse] [I deserve all this] [everything is my fault]

[I let people down] [I can't trust you] [why do I try?] [don't you dare cry] [I'm scared of myself]

[I am constantly terrified] [I push everyone away] [love must be earned] [I am not worthy] [I try so hard]

[You really hurt me] [The world is scary] [life is a contradiction] [Is it only me?] [people hide the truth] [just let me die]

[I'm in unbearable pain] [I can't trust anyone] [What if you leave?] [I have no voice] [nothing is ever fair]

[People expect too much] [I cause my problems]

[my heart is aching] [I feel so alone] [no one really cares] [nothing helps me anymore]

[I'm too tired now] [my wrists are burning] [I'm alone in this] [you still haunt me]

[what is happiness anyway?] [No one really understands] [emotions make you weak]

[people don't like me] [my pain is irrelevant] [this will last forever] [Please help me through] [no one listens properly]

[We all die anyway] [I can't feel anything]

[lying is just easier] [I'm only safe alone] [my life is worthless] [I'm easy to ignore]

[I have no reason] [bad attention's still attention]

143

It's okay
if all
you did
today
was
survive

Inner child affirmations
- I am safe and loved
- my feelings are valid
- I deserve happiness
- I can control how I respond
- I show myself compassion
- I am protected
- I have resilience
- I am enough
- I can manage emotions

Trust

Guilt

• Inner child wounds •

Neglect

Abandonment

Healing your inner child...

This isn't your fault

Find a safe place
Be non-judgemental

Apologise to yourself

Remind yourself of your strengths

Protect yourself

you're there for them

Tell your inner child that you love them

Acknowledge that your inner child may be hurt, scared etc. and comfort them

Visualise caring for them

Say things you wish others had said

I NNER CHILD

Signs of a hurt inner child
- low self esteem
- People-pleasing
- Self-destructive behaviour
- Social anxiety
- jealousy
- untrusting
- dependency issues
- difficulty communicating
- Issues with anger
- Trouble letting go
- Struggles with commitment
- reduced decision making ability

Encourage yourself

Acknowledge your good qualities

Release blame

Self-care

Validate yourself

pursue your interests

Re-parenting your inner child

use affirmations

Play games

'is this behaviour harmful or helpful?'

Set limits and boundaries

Identify your feelings

Ways to support and co-exist with your inner child:

- Reassure them that you are working on healing the wounds from your past
- Introduce them to your current self ; an independent adult that is capable of fulfilling both your needs
- Show them the new, safe coping mechanisms you can use now

Validate their feelings
Give them permission to have fun

Restructuring your thinking. examples :

wounded inner child	loving inner parent
Everything is my fault	People make mistakes and that's okay
I'll never be good enough	I'm learning to accept myself and will be gentle with myself
I don't deserve ... (eg. rest)	how can I take care of myself right now?
everything is falling apart	this is a moment of suffering that will pass

inner child

As a child, it was not your responsibility to:

- manage your parents' emotions
- provide safety and security for yourself
- raise younger / older siblings
- face emotional struggles alone
- resolve problems faced by older, adult family members

People-please to feel valued or loved

"Anything that is "wrong" with you began as a survival mechanism in childhood."

— Dr Gabor Maté

TYPES OF EXERCISE

Aerobic
Balance and Stability
Coordination and agility
Flexibility and mobility
Strength training

Physical health benefits of exercise

⬇ disease risk

⬆ bone strength

⬆ brain health

⬆ Weight loss

⬇ blood pressure

⬆ sleep quality

⬆ memory

⬇ risk of heart attack

THE BENEFITS OF PHYSICAL ACTIVITY on

MENTAL HEALTH

physiological mechanisms benefit mental state e.g. stimulate neuroplastic processes

Improves mental wellbeing and reduces anxiety

Reduces risk of developing mental illness

Better cognitive health and performance

Emotional resilience

Reduced physiological distress

Emotional regulation

Lower levels of stress

Reduces the intensity of existing depression and anxiety

Promotes social interaction

Improves self-esteem

Understanding your emotions

The function of emotions

- emotions are primal and occur when something occurs involving our physical senses, promoting physical survival.
- There are primary emotions which have specific functions, and a range of their own secondary emotions which are emotional responses to emotions
- emotions impact our behaviour, so therefore have a wider effect on those around us
- Secondary emotions are learned, not innate

Fear

- can be experienced as a thought, feeling or behaviour
- responses can be fight, flight or freeze
- can be expressed passively or aggressively
- extreme form = terror
- can lead to destructive anger or depression

Anger

- occurs in response to a crossing of boundaries, abuse, threats to our inner sense of justice, or as a secondary emotion to fear
- extreme form = rage
- repressed = depression
- responses can be assertive, aggressive, or passive
- can lead to behaviours like addiction or violence

Secondary emotions

Secondary → Primary

Shame with anger

anger with shame

Fear with anger

anxiety with mania

depression with fear

guilt with anxiety

inadequacy with sadness

anger with rejection

trust with happiness

Shame with vulnerability

To address the secondary emotion it is necessary to identify the underlying emotion and challenge that.

Sadness

- contextual, caused by happiness
- can occur due to loss; e.g. grief, separation anxiety, loss of safety
- allows us to acknowledge someone or something of value
- can be experienced in extreme forms (mania or depression)
- abuse can lead to feelings of guilt or shame in place of sadness

Happiness

- generates a quality of life to rebalance with negative emotion
- improve relationships
- defined differently by everyone
- joy or absence of pain?
- may feel unjustified
- unhealthy relationship to emotions can lead to euphoria or numbness

May the
blowers
remind us why the
rain was so
necessary

-XAN OKU

Dissociation = a disconnect from sensory experience, thoughts, feelings, memories, and sense of self.

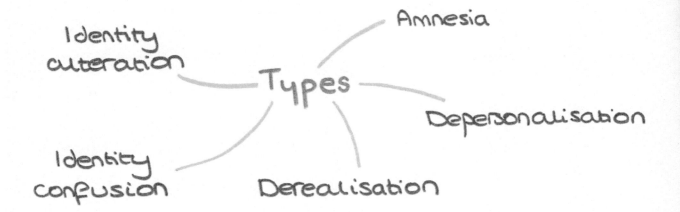

Identity
alteration

Amnesia

Types

Depersonalisation

Identity
confusion

Derealisation

Disconnection a

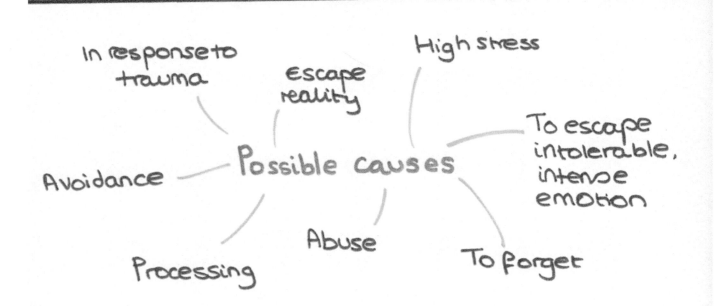

In response to
trauma

High stress

escape
reality

To escape
intolerable,
intense
emotion

Avoidance — Possible causes

Abuse

To forget

Processing

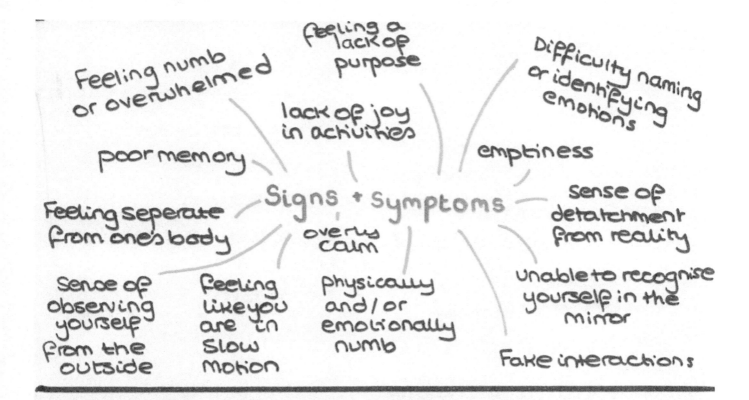

Signs + Symptoms

- Feeling numb or overwhelmed
- Feeling a lack of purpose
- Difficulty naming or identifying emotions
- lack of joy in activities
- emptiness
- poor memory
- sense of detatchment from reality
- Feeling seperate from one's body
- over ly calm
- Sense of observing yourself from the outside
- Feeling like you are in slow motion
- physically and/or emotionally numb
- Unable to recognise yourself in the mirror
- Fake interactions

nd dissociation

Tips to cope

- Seek help through therapy to address the underlying cause
- Engage your senses
- meditation
- Grounding
- Mindfulness
- Deep breathing
- Get enough sleep
- Be kind and patient with yourself

Types:

- Amnesia
  - lack of recollection of a particular instance
- depersonalisation
  - out of body experiences
- derealisation
  - distorted reality
- Identity confusion or alteration
  - uncertainty or change

Why?

- protection from trauma
- Stress reduction
- avoidance
- distraction
- response to overwhelming stimuli
- processing
- to numb emotions

Dissociation + disconnect

out of body experience

forgetting events or personal information

disconnected from the world/reality

feel like you're floating

feeling numb

difficulties recollecting from this time

detatched from the present

can feel like a different person

far off gaze

Signs

feel your heart pounding and/or lightheaded

emotionally numb

feel little to no pain

observe yourself from outside your body

lacking purpose

lack of emotion/ burying emotions

lack control of your body

I'm still learning

I have the right to set and maintain my own boundaries

The importance of being patient with myself

There can be growth in stillness

Pausing for a break doesn't equal failure

Relying on others to make me happy also gives them the power to hurt me or for me to feel let down

Asking for help is okay

The slightest progress, or even preventing decline, is still growth

Just because I am struggling, doesn't mean I'm weak

Sometimes doing nothing is still productive. It allows time to re-gain energy and reflect.

My best is enough

necessary rest isn't laziness

my healing doesn't have to look like others'

I can't control how others respond to me

THINGS...

I'm unlearning

Not to ignore my own boundaries or needs in order to please others

I don't have to know what the future will look like to work on myself in the present

changing myself to fit in to social situations

self-worth isn't dependent on productivity

The only healthy unconditional love is parent to child

To not pretend I'm okay and avoid seeking support

That silencing myself and compromising my values in order to save from conflict

Society and culture have many unrealistic expectations for appearance and health

Not acknowledging my success, or my struggles as others have it worse

Self assurance is healthier than external validation

processing difficult feelings is better in the long term

THE CYCLE OF SELF HARM

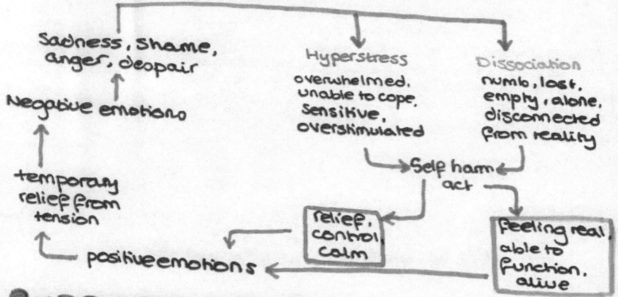

Sadness, Shame, anger, despair

Negative emotions

temporary relief from tension

positive emotions

Hyperstress
overwhelmed, unable to cope, sensitive, overstimulated

Dissociation
numb, lost, empty, alone, disconnected from reality

Self harm act

relief, control, calm

feeling real, able to function, alive

SUPPORTING SOMEONE

Don't panic
- Stay calm
- be kind

Talk
- don't demand info
- encourage sharing feelings

Don't punish
- This isn't disobedience
- The individually is emotionally vulnerable. Treat them nicely

Assess the Situation
- offer care, support, first aid

Check yourself
- do you need support?

Pay attention
- Don't be over-bearing, but be aware of increased suicide risk

Therapy
- consider a referral for them/you

Harm reduction
- make the environment safer
- encourage openness
- Be available to support
- recovery

All my love
– okaywill

Electric Love
– BØRNS

Let's dance to
Joy Division
– The Wombats

Fight on
– The Lathums

Invincible
– Two door cinema club

Australia
– The Shins

Dreamers
– Neon Waltz

Just hold on
– Steve Aoki

Problems
– Dylan John
Thomas

This is Gospel
– Panic! At the
Disco

Change my Love
– Craig David

Flammable
– Biffy Clyro

Wild Flowers
– Frank Carter
& The
Rattlesnakes

I Better Love You
– Will Heard

Real stuff
– Leif Erikson

Do You Love Someone
– Grouplove

Take it from me
– Konaos

I Always
Knew
– The
Vaccines

Everybody Talks
– Neon Trees

100 Times Over
– Cassia

MOOD BOOST MIXTAPE

Calm
– Vistas

Adore You
– Harry
Styles

Plug In
Baby
– Muse

Oh my Love
– The Lathums

All we Ever Knew
– The Head and The
Heart

I Bet You Look
Good On The
Dancefloor
– Arctic Monkeys

End of the World
– Fatherson

Cheer Up Baby
– Inhaler

Call me Out
– Sea Girls

Sometimes
– Gerry Cinnamon

Circles
– Alfie
Templeman

Kathleen
– Catfish and the
Bottlemen

Take Back
The Track
– The
Magic
Gang

Drifting
– Cassia

T-shirt Weather
– Circa Waves

She Said
– Sundara Karma

The Love you give
– Vistas

Go Outside
– Viola Beach

Dreaming of you
– The Coral

Toothpaste
Kisses
– The
Maccabees

This Life
– Vampire
weekend

Better Together
– Jack Johnson

Loving is easy
– Rex Orange County

How can I compete
– The magic gang

Sun Queen – Gerry Cinnamon

Attatchment types

Secure

- confident
- resilient
- healthy communication
- able to ask for help
- reciprocal
- can self-regulate
- trusts fairly easily
- co-operative in relationships

Avoidant

- Isolating
- ambiguous
- emotional distance
- difficulty expressing emotion
- struggle asking for help
- wants but afraid of intimacy
- untrusting

Anxious

- fear abandonment
- require reassurance
- struggles to communicate
- tends to "act out"
- easily triggered
- dependent
- anxious
- chronic survival mode

Disorganised

- anxious + avoidant traits
- fear rejection but intimacy issues
- low self esteem
- trouble recognising emotions
- disconnected sense of self
- fear of rejection
- misunderstanding of love

There are days when I wish I hadn't woken up. These are the hardest days. These are the days where I feel terrified and alone. These are the days in which I'm desperate for help, but don't know how to ask for it. These are the days in which I force a smile, carry on. These are the days that push me to the edge, and threaten my existence. These are the days that are becoming my everyday.

I know no one else can save me, and that I have to save myself. But I really don't want to have to do all this alone. I'm terrified and battling so hard to stay afloat. So please, hold my hand, while I work to make myself better. I can't

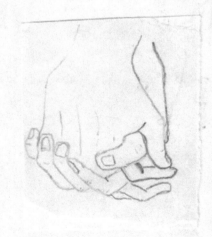

do this on my own, the world is a scary, lonely place. But nothing compared to the state of my mind. I can't go on being isolated in my own head.

'I know this
transformation is
painful, but you're not
falling apart;
you're just falling into
Something different,
With a new
Capacity
to be beautiful'

— William C. Hannan

GASLIGHTING CAN LOOK LIKE...

Gaslighting = a form of manipulation and abuse in which the victim doubts reality

'I never said that'

'I never did that'

'you're lying!'

lying and covering up the truth
----
denial

defensive | intentional wrong
false | placement
accusations | of blame

leads to questioning of thoughts, memories, events, and reality

Implications of insanity, "crazy", stupidity

'you're so...
sensitive
emotional
dramatic

Getting others to see the victim differently

Actions that are contradictory to words
----
convince someone that they are imagining things
----
unsupportive

Broken promises | projection and guilt tripping

They're going to hurt you

No one is bothered by how you feel

The future is scary

If you go to sleep, you'll have nightmares

Everyone is mad at you.

No one cares

Shut up

You're weak

Take an overdose

why can't you just be okay?

You should be more than this

You are a failure

You're letting everyone down

you're a burden

everyone is judging you

Everyone hates you

you're so fat

You're beyond help

Hurt yourself

you look ugly

Do it, you're dull

Remember all the bad things you've ever done? Lets go through them all. You can't do this

ALL THE THOUGHTS IN MY MIND AT ANY ONE TIME

What's the point?

you're an embarrassment

They're going to leave

you are pathetic

You've forgotten...

You've definitely forgotten...

you and everyone else would be better off if you weren't around

Just end it all.

They're talking about you

Don't cry. Don't cry. Don't cry.

You've let everyone down

This is all your fault

life is terrible

Everything is your fault

you deserve to feel like this

you make bad choices

Don't be so selfish

you've brought this upon yourself

you're self-centred

No one likes you

Nobody wants to spend time with you

you are boring

Why do you even bother when you fuck everything up anyway?

What you want and need is irrelevant

people feel obliged to care about you

you're hard work

you'll never get better

you'll never achieve anything

you are unloveable

161

Assuming that because I am feeling a certain way, that it must be true	Seeing a pattern based on a single event, or drawing very broad conclusions	Giving labels to ourselves, other people, and situations
Emotional reasoning	**Overgeneralising**	**Labelling**
Jumping to conclusions	**All or nothing**	**Should/must**
two main types: mind reading and fortune telling. The latter involves making predictions about the future.	Also called 'black or white' thinking. No middle ground. e.g. entirely good or entirely bad	critical and demanding. can lead to feelings of guilt or failure. when applied to others it can cause frustration.
Placing blame or taking responsibility for something that's not entirely your fault	Blowing things out of proportion or making something seem less important than it is	Only paying attention to certain types of evidence that fit our beliefs/emotions
Personalisation	**Catastrophising**	**Mental filter**
discounting good things that have happened or you've done	A form of catastrophising that involves 'making a mountain out of a mole hill'	A form of 'jumping to conclusion' thinking style. Imagining we know what others are thinking.
Disqualifying positives	**magnification**	**Mind reading**
Comparison	**Self criticism**	**Perfectionism**
comparing directly against others, or their good traits with our imperfections (or perceived imperfections)	putting ourselves down. A combination of negative thinking styles (personalisation, comparison, should/must)	A small mistake can be perceived as complete failure. Unrealistic, high expectations of self or others.

UNHELPFUL THINKING

The stars nodded,
The ocean agreed,
The flowers chorused,
"Bloom now - bloom free".
- rise again

Tess Guinery

Feel your feelings

Not feeling good → What is it I am feeling → Where am I feeling it? → How would I verbalise it?

↓

What might this feeling be telling me?

Allow yourself to feel, cry if you need to ← What steps can I take? ← What do I need? ←

Set boundaries (examples)

My values	So I need to...	Maintaining the boundary
my emotional wellbeing	learn to say 'no' sometimes	not allow others to persuade me into a 'yes'
personal growth	test my limits	use what I learn and recognise my bravery
equality	treat all people with respect	uphold respect even through adversity

Make progress

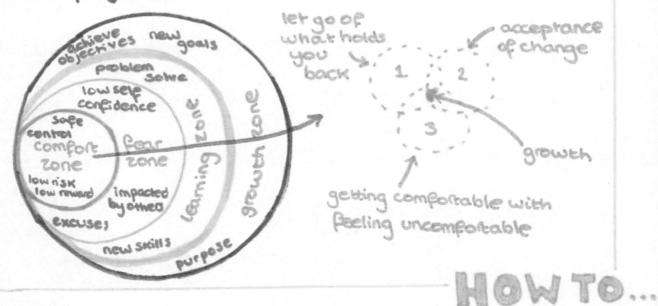

achieve objectives new goals

problem solve

low self confidence

safe control

comfort zone

fear zone

low risk low reward

impacted by others

excuses

new skills

learning zone

growth zone

purpose

let go of what holds you back

acceptance of change

1   2

3

growth

getting comfortable with feeling uncomfortable

HOW TO...

164

MISTAKES ARE PROOF THAT YOU'RE TRYING

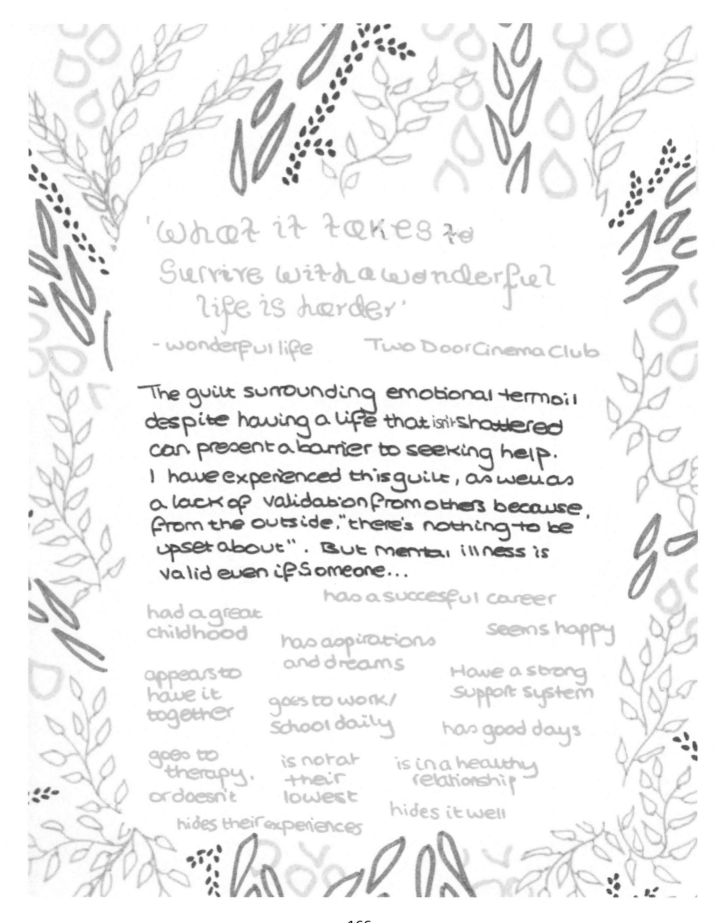

'What it takes to
Survive with a wonderful
life is harder'
- Wonderful life   Two Door Cinema Club

The guilt surrounding emotional turmoil
despite having a life that isn't shattered
can present a barrier to seeking help.
I have experienced this guilt, as well as
a lack of validation from others because,
from the outside, "there's nothing to be
upset about". But mental illness is
valid even if someone...

had a great   has a successful career
childhood
                has aspirations   seems happy
                and dreams
appears to   Have a strong
have it   goes to work/   support system
together   school daily
                                   has good days
goes to   is not at   is in a healthy
    therapy.   their   relationship
or doesn't   lowest
                               hides it well
hides their experiences

You drained me of my identity
and injected self doubt
into my veins
Left me questioning my own
Sanity
Walking around aimlessly
At war with my own body
every day
Trying to scrub your heavy
words off my skin
My mental state has been
Shaken to its core
I don't know who I am anymore

e.s.

Forgiveness

Self-forgiveness:

- I am going to make mistakes but that's okay because I am trying, growing, and learning

- I can be patient with myself, and forgive my past mistakes and decisions when justified

- I will try to practice letting go of self-criticism and self-judgement

- I will work on changing my negative thought patterns and behaviours, and forgive my previous treatment of myself

Forgiving others:

- Even if they aren't necessarily right, or don't offer an apology, forgiveness allows you to move on for yourself

'Keep in mind that forgiving is not for others. It is for you. Forgiving is not forgetting. It is remembering without anger. It frees up your power, heals your body, mind and spirit. Forgiveness opens up a pathway to a new place of peace'

Les Brown

- Forgiving those who have done wrong to us means we can release any negative emotions that weigh us down. Remember that others' emotional intelligence (or lack of) can prevent an apology

- Healing connection with those we want to maintain the relationship with, or re-affirming faith in others, are just some of what we stand to achieve

Daily tasks I find challenging and why...

Seeing friends
- worrying they secretly don't like me
- anxious
- exhaustion from the effort of socialising
- Not wanting to be boring or miserable
- Thinking I'm annoying and they'd rather be elsewhere
- Not wanting to let them down

Intense Exercise
- racing heart — can prompt my body to think it's having a panic attack due to similar body sensations
- Sweating
- Shortness of breath

Commute by train
- overwhelming
- worry I will be attacked, there will be an accident with the train, or I have a panic attack in public

Grocery Shopping
- overwhelming
- memory problems
- poor concentration
- anxious
- busy

Eating at a restaurant
- everyone knows I'm unwell
- pressure to choose
- convinced I'm unsafe

Cooking
- what if I get food poisoning?
- requires lots of effort and I have no energy

Driving
- what if I crash?
- am I safe when I'm sad or anxious?
- What if I get lost?
- What if I break down?
- thinking too much to be able to concentrate

Keeping up with world news
- makes me sadder
- The world scares me
- It seems we're all doomed
- requires a lot of energy
- easily distracted

Watching TV, reading a book, listening to music
- tired from focusing

Cleaning + hoovering + ironing
- wanting a tidy space but the thought of tidying is overwhelming

Walking the dog
- what if we get lost?
- my mind wonders and thoughts snowball into a negative spiral
- what if the dog runs off or gets hurt
- too much time alone leads to over-thinking
- what if someone is rude or attacks me?

169

EMOTION EQUATIONS

Sadness = Hope - reality + pain

Anger = Perception + threat

Anxiety = Anticipation + negative thinking

Happiness = Safety + authenticity

Regret = Morals - responsibility

Fear = Experience - safety

Comfort = protection + sympathy

Self-esteem = confidence + experience

Trust = Expectation + vulnerability

Untrusting = Fear + experience

Perfectionism = Priorities - self-care + expectations

Belonging = inclusion + similarity

Narcissism = Self-esteem - empathy

People-pleasing = compromise + discomfort + perceived obligation

Confusion = Perception - truth

Lonliness = comfort - belonging - company

SIGNS

UNREALISTIC EXPECTATIONS

POOR CONCENTRATION

OVERTHINKING

PEOPLE PLEASING

SWEATING

ORGANISED

AVOIDANCE

UPSET STOMACH

MEMORY ISSUES

IRRITABLE

PANIC ATTACKS

IMPATIENT

OVERWORKING

NEGLECT OF SELF

SEEKING REASSURANCE

TROUBLE BREATHING

PROCRASTINATION

HEADACHES

RAPID HEART RATE

PERSISTENT WORRY

INSOMNIA

BUSY

OVERACHIEVING

"YES" PERSON

SELF-CRITICISM

PERFECTIONISM

FEAR OF DISAPPOINTING OTHERS

DIZZY

RUMINATION

MENTAL EXHAUSTION

ANXIETY CAN LOOK LIKE

WITHDRAWN

SOCIAL ISOLATION

LOW SELF ESTEEM

DREAD

DISLIKING BEING CENTRE OF ATTENTION

SHY

UNABLE TO SAY 'NO'

NEED FOR EXTERNAL VALIDATION

PHYSICAL FATIGUE

INTERNAL

EXTERNAL

What you see	How it feels	
Punctuality	Paranoid about lateness	COMPARISON WITH OTHERS
High achieving	Terrified of failure	
Well prepared	Overthinking and planning	PHYSICAL DISCOMFORT
Organised	Avoiding loss of control or being overwhelmed	
		NOT IN THE PRESENT MOMENT
Helpful + caring	Fear of rejection	
Relaxed	Internalised emotions	SENSITIVE
		PROACTIVE
Confident	Over-exertion and trying to convince self/others	
		DIFFICULTY ASKING FOR HELP

172

depression

Perfectionism

All or nothing — do a task well or not at all

Trying again — seek feeling worth in environment

Intense drive — work is driven by feelings of imperfection and flaws. Fear of dissatisfaction.

depression — feel inadequate and a failure. Overwhelmed

Burnout — overworked, reject self-care.

Can occur as high functioning depression. over-compensation for feelings of worthlessness and perceived flaws.

my experience

I wake up every morning and feel overwhelmed by the thought of facing the day.

I find no enjoyment in anything, at most I won't be as sad. I struggle to look forward to anything as I become intensely anxious and just want to hide from the world

I feel a weight on my chest constantly. It makes breathing difficult and every movement an effort.

Trying to get better takes a motivation I barely possess. I also don't know what happy looks like, so I don't know what I'm aiming for.

I disguise how I feel all the time, otherwise I break and can't stop the tears.

My heart aches with an inexplicable despair and desperation. I have no faith or hope left and the world terrifies me. everything feels pointless, as I'm likely to get hurt anyway.

The downward spiral of depression

Negative experience

suppressed emotions

repetitive negative thinking

physical distress

avoidance + unhelpful behaviour

uncontrolled depression

Ongoing internal conflicts

Needing and wanting connections with friends and family

No energy to talk or socialise. Fear of being bad company

wanting comfort and people around

wanting to be alone

Not wanting to feel like this

Insomnia

exhaustion

Knowing coping strategies

No motivation to get better

No motivation or energy to do or use them

wanting to seek support

worrying about being a burden

Indecisive

need for consistency and/or control

excessive worry

not caring about anything

174

Look for the light in the Storm

MEANINGFUL

You should be really proud of yourself. I'm proud of you	I always learn so much from you
You're a great listener. I always feel seen and heard by you	I admire you	I really like how creative you are
Your work ethic is so inspirational	I appreciate how open you are with me	You have such a kind heart
You bring out the best in me	I trust you and can depend on you	

COMPLIMENTS

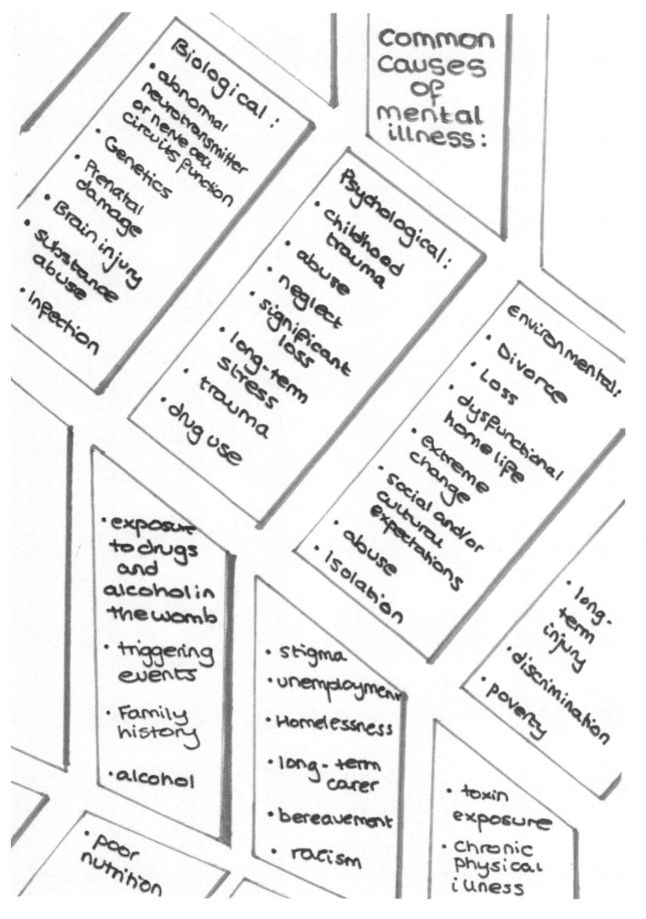

Common Causes of mental illness:

Biological:
- abnormal neurotransmitter or nerve cell circuits function
- Genetics
- Prenatal damage
- Brain injury
- Substance abuse
- Infection

Psychological:
- childhood trauma
- abuse
- neglect
- significant loss
- long-term stress
- trauma
- drug use

Environmental:
- Divorce
- Loss
- dysfunctional home life
- extreme change
- social and/or cultural expectations
- abuse
- Isolation

- exposure to drugs and alcohol in the womb
- triggering events
- Family history
- alcohol

- stigma
- unemployment
- Homelessness
- long-term carer
- bereavement
- racism

- long-term injury
- discrimination
- poverty

- toxin exposure
- Chronic physical illness

- poor nutrition

'ADOPT THE PACE OF NATURE. HER SECRET IS PATIENCE.' - Ralph Waldo Emerson

'IN EVERY WALK WITH NATURE ONE RECEIVES FAR MORE THAN HE SEEKS' - John Muir

'NATURE IS THE PUREST PORTAL TO INNER-PEACE'
- Angie Weiland Crosby

Depression + anxiety

A common combination, but no less difficult to experience and navigate. It would be reasonable to presume, as an outside perspective, that the two help balance each other out. Unfortunately not the case.

Examples of how depression and anxiety struggle to co-exist in my mind:

- caring about everything and nothing all at once
- doubt and fear alongside a lack of trust, but not being bothered what happens to you because you don't matter anyway
- exhaustion emotionally and physically, but using any extra energy to over-analyse and worry about real or hypothetical situations
- anxiety imposes with skepticism and concern about people, ourselves, and events. Depression then backs this up with negative perspectives and (often tenuous) evidence.
- panic but apathetic
- hypervigilance but lethargic
- uncertainty of how to behave and think

MASLOW'S HIERARCHY OF NEEDS

Self
actualisation
Achieving full potential

Accomplishment prestige
Esteem
Skill acquisition recognition

Intimacy Friendships
Love + belonging
Relationships Affiliation

order protection Law
Security Safety morality
Stability

sex food water sleep
air Physiological needs
shelter nest warmth hygiene health

PROBLEM SOLVING SKILLS

Bloom's Taxonomy

create
Evaluate
Analyse
Apply
understand
Remember

Continuous improvement

Identify the problem
gather info/data
Continue to improve
analyse
implement
plan
Select a solution
generate solutions

Important safety plan details for times of crisis, that can be quickly referred to and put in place.

CRISIS PLAN

Coping skills:
- ☐
- ☐
- ☐

distractions:

1

2

3

4

Triggers and warning Signs:

_____

_____

people I can contact:

- .
- .
- .
- .

Ways to keep myself and my space safe : _ _ _ _ _ _
_ _ _ _ _ _ _ _ _ _ _ _ _

resources and numbers to call:

☐ ☐ ☐ ☐

How our beliefs lead to our "rules to live by"

Beliefs develop from how we are treated, how our behaviours produce certain outcomes, and how we perceive ourselves. These influence each other and intertwine to govern our morals, actions, and "rules to live by"

Belief	"Rule"
showing emotions is weak	do NOT show emotion
people are manipulative and have hidden agendas	Don't trust people until I'm sure
I'm fat	I don't deserve to eat

My "rules to live by"

Belief	"rule"
everyone will let me down at some point	don't rely on anyone
The world is scary	Be cautious
I'm weak and can't cope when I get hurt	Life isn't worth living

My beliefs and "rules"

Belief	"rule"
seeking support is a sign of weakness	struggle alone
I can't do anything right	be perfect to compensate
My struggles are my fault and I deserve them	punish myself

Further examples

'believe in yourself and all that you are. know that there is something inside you that is greater than any obstacle'
-Christian D. Larson

She didn't want to be saved. She needed to be found and appreciated for exactly who she was.

- J. Ironword

Thank them for telling you → Ask what triggered them → Attempt to understand what they're communicating

↓ (left side flow)

If lives are at risk, go to A+E

↑

If needed, contact a healthcare / psychological professional

Work through or create a safety plan

↑

Seek resources or further support

↑

Praise their strength ←

Explain their worth etc. ← Express belief in them. Gain trust.

↓ ↑

Encourage the use of coping techniques and emotion regulation

↓

Gently challenge their negative or self-critical thoughts

emotional appeal for communication

↑

Try to read their body language

↑

Check-in with yourself. Do you need to seek more help? ←

Validate

↓

Show concern, not void of response

↓

encourage openness

↓

diffuse the intensity of the emotion by taking a break e.g. go for a walk

↓

Remove triggers and potentially harmful items

RESPONDING TO SOMEONE IN CRISIS

BE KIND
Follow through
create a plan
Explore options
Process emotion
Identify the trigger
Build trust
Assess the crisis

Helping with immediate recovery...

- distraction
- relaxation
- Further help needed?
- Face triggers if appropriate

Assess risk

- Physical
  - Self harm?
  - Safe enviroment?
  - Other injury?
- emotional / psychological
  - triggers?
  - suicidal?
  - how can their distress be reduced?
  - extent of risk to self and/or others

'I'm not interested in whether you've stood with the great. I'm interested in whether you've sat with the broken'
    – Sue Fitzmaurice

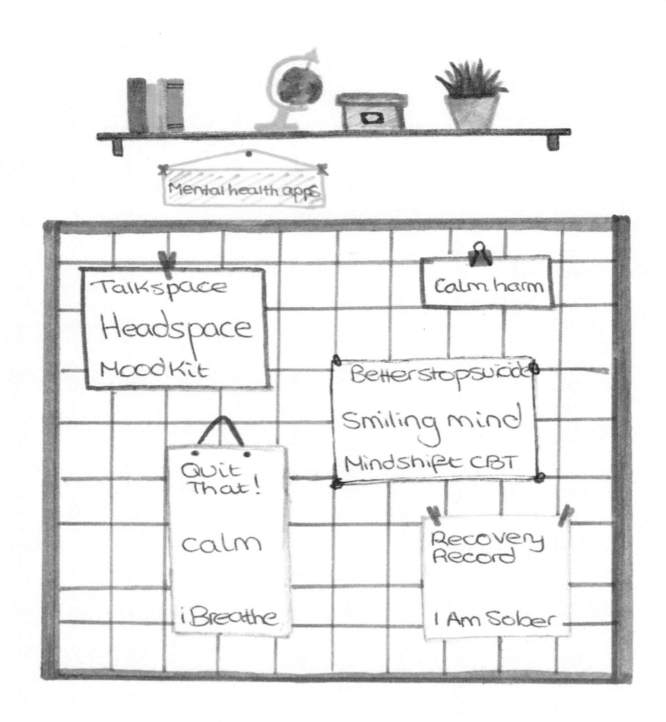

If you could read my mind, you'd be in tears

tears are words the heart can't say

People cry not because they're weak. It's because they've been strong for too long.

— Johnny Depp

It hurts, but it's okay. I'm used to it.

Broken People Understand Broken People.

HOW DO I EXPLAIN THIS?

Head up Stay Strong fake a smile move on

I am trying my hardest not to act like how I feel

Burnout happens when you avoid being human for too long

hanginthere

My Mental Illness Pinterest Board

I can't tell if it's killing me or making me stronger.

Some say I'm too sensitive. But I just feel too much. Every word, every action, goes straight to my heart.

Just because someone carries it well, doesn't mean it isn't heavy.

—·—·—·—·—

Sleep doesn't help if it's your soul that's tired.

I'm drowning without the water.

Pain changes you

You wake up every morning to fight the same demons that left you so tired the night before and that, my love, is bravery.

THE ONLY THING MORE EXHAUSTING THAN BEING DEPRESSED IS PRETENDING YOU'RE NOT

It hurts. It hurts a lot. But I'll keep it to myself so it doesn't hurt anyone else

Silent tears hold the loudest pain

-'How do you feel?'

-'I don't.'

I WORE A MASK FOR SO LONG, I DON'T KNOW WHO I AM ANYMORE

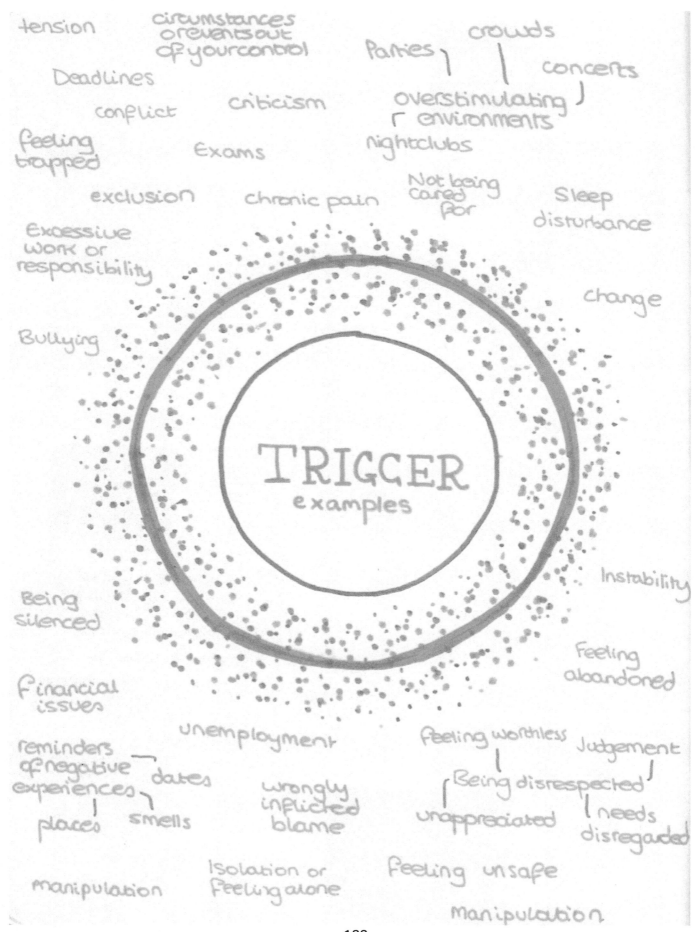

tension

circumstances or events out of your control

Parties

crowds

concerts

Deadlines

criticism

overstimulating environments

conflict

nightclubs

feeling trapped

Exams

exclusion

chronic pain

Not being cared for

Sleep disturbance

Excessive work or responsibility

change

Bullying

TRIGGER

examples

Instability

Being silenced

Feeling abandoned

Financial issues

unemployment

feeling worthless

Judgement

reminders of negative experiences

dates

wrongly inflicted blame

Being disrespected

places

smells

unappreciated

needs disregarded

manipulation

Isolation or feeling alone

feeling unsafe

manipulation

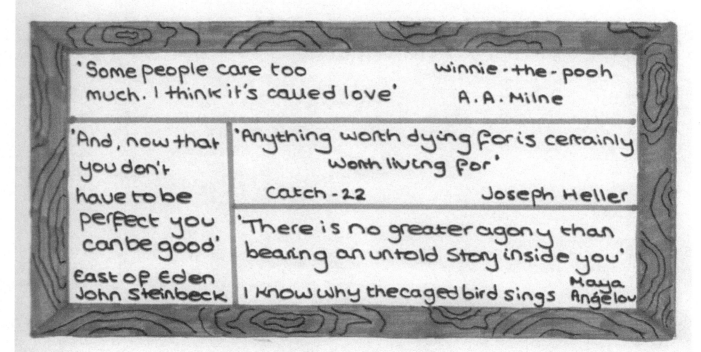

'Some people care too much. I think it's called love'
winnie-the-pooh
A.A. Milne

'And, now that you don't have to be perfect you can be good'
East of Eden
John Steinbeck

'Anything worth dying for is certainly worth living for'
Catch-22
Joseph Heller

'There is no greater agony than bearing an untold story inside you'
I know why the caged bird sings
Maya Angelou

QUOTES

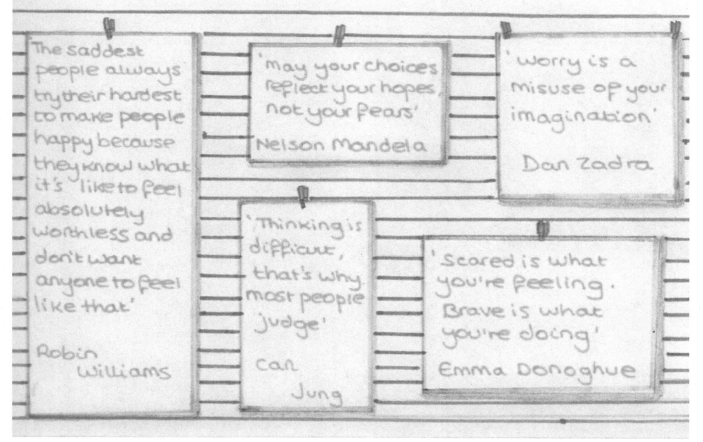

'The saddest people always try their hardest to make people happy because they know what it's like to feel absolutely worthless and don't want anyone to feel like that'
Robin Williams

'may your choices reflect your hopes, not your fears'
Nelson Mandela

'worry is a misuse of your imagination'
Dan Zadra

'Thinking is difficult, that's why most people judge'
Carl Jung

'Scared is what you're feeling. Brave is what you're doing'
Emma Donoghue

whether you want to start a conversation about your own mental health, encourage someone who is struggling to open up, or inspire a supportive environment in the workplace and elsewhere, it is the initiation of the conversation that can set the tone as one of supportive concern or unintended criticism and invalidation. Therefore it is necessary to proceed with discretion in order to develop a safe space that advocates trust and confidentiality.

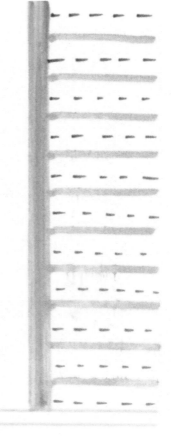

Starting the conversation...

Tips

- a suitable time and place
- quiet, undisturbed space
- don't expect too much too soon
- show respect
- a method of communication most effective for you
- do not rush
- plan what you want to say
- suggest ways to help you or to help them
- do your research, understand yourself / others and find resources to help to be understood or support someone else
- be honest but don't share anything you don't feel comfortable sharing yet

The benefits

+ could gain support
+ it shows strength
+ encourages others to open up
+ to be understood
+ can get things off your mind
+ helps others to understand mental health in general
+ problem solving

The worry tree

Notice the worry
↓
Is there anything I can do about the situation

No / Yes

No → let the worry go → Focus attention elsewhere

Yes → What? When? How? → Make a change or plan for it

Therapy timetable

M	T	W	T	F	S	S

Type: _____ Time: _____

· Experience it
· Distress tolerance techniques
· Distraction
· Mindfulness
· Talk it through

How are you?

[Pause]
1 What emotion(s) are present?
2 Any bodily sensations?
3 Where could these emotions be coming from?
4 What can you do to improve the moment?

MENTAL HEALTH CHECK-IN

How was your day?
Amazing : 10 → Terrible : 1

M AM ☐ PM ☐
Why? _____

T AM ☐ PM ☐
Why? _____

W AM ☐ PM ☐
Why? _____

T AM ☐ PM ☐
Why? _____

F AM ☐ PM ☐
Why? _____

What's on your mind?

express   manage emotions
                        prioritise
reflect   observe
                  acceptance
find meaning
                                respect
feel   understand   yourself

♥ Don't forget the good parts ♥
★ what are you grateful for?
★ what/who made you smile today?
★ Think about your happy place
★ What was good about today?
★ You got through the day ♥

the
PerKs of
being a
wallflower

FIGHT CLUB

One Flew Over the Cuckoo's Nest | *American Beauty* | *Black Swan*

THE KING'S SPEECH

LITTLE MISS SUNSHINE

IT'S A WONDERFUL LIFE

MENTAL ILLNESS IN THE MOVIES

FEAR   JOY

DISGUST   INSIDE OUT

ANGER   SADNESS

Silver Lining Playbook | A Beautiful Mind | Girl, Interrupted | Shutter Island

Warning signs:
- low motivation
- Insomnia + fatigue
- Anxious
- Emotionally overwhelmed
- Poor physical health
- Irritable
- Feeling like a failure

Contributors:
- unrealistic expectations of self
- Ignoring own needs
- Social withdrawal
- overworking
- denial
- neglecting down time
- repressing emotions
- people pleasing

Burnout...

emotional exhaustion:
- helplessness
- numb / detatched
- poor concentration
- actions based on obligation
- lack of joy or happiness
- pessimism
- withdrawn
- emotional outbursts
- fatigue

Signs of recovery:
- Recognising triggers
- Implementing self-care and routine
- setting boundaries
- well-rounded lifestyle
- drive and ambition

Ways to heal:
- time to rest or get away
- time in nature
- exercise
- healthy diet
- target cause
- develop resilience skills

Mental Health FAQs ?

What is the difference between a psychiatrist and a psychologist?

psychiatrist :
- medically-qualified practitioner
- further training after general medicine
- can prescribe medication
- can diagnose and treat psychological problems

psychologist :
- Have a relevant degree, but not usually medically trained
- Study and work on how people think, act, behave, and interact

Is medication or therapy a better treatment option?

medication isn't typically the first treatment option for mild cases.

Therapy can be based on different models and is more readily available. medication can help individuals engage better with therapy in more severe cases.

Can you prevent mental health problems?

Though problems can't be fully prevented, and suffering isn't a personal "failure" or fault, developing resilience and emotional wellbeing can help keep struggles at bay

How do I know if my mental health is suffering?

A good indication that you are emotionally struggling is if your thoughts, behaviours, beliefs and feelings are having a significant negative impact on your normal day-to-day functioning ability

Who is most at risk of mental illness?

Young adults (18 to 25) have the highest prevalence. other high risk groups are : LGBTQ+, BAME, homeless, young women,

Hidden depression

I have experienced all of these, making depression very challenging. However, I haven't felt denial, but can sympathise with how it could occur in order to cope

Hiding from others

Nothing hurts more than trying your best to still end up not being "good enough". So hiding your "flaws" can feel like a way of presenting yourself more favourably.

Shame, guilt, and pride are just some of the feelings that can prevent someone from opening up.

Because it is a mental illness, there is sometimes a perception that it is "chosen" to be shown and can be turned off when needed. But it is always there, and masking it to avoid judgement or ridicule doesn't make it any easier. Its not "all in your head".

To avoid being a (perceived) burden.

Fear of becoming judged or treated differently

Denial and/or numbing

- Intense focus on tasks and taking on excessive responsibility, in order to distract from emotions
- Imposter syndrome
- Secret coping mechanisms
- Not seeking help or support
- maintaining a facade
  ↳ to the extent that it feels real, despite feeling nothing by blocking out all emotion, even the good ones

- Addiction
- Avoidance
- Social withdrawal
- Emotionless
- Distraction
- Lack of emotional response to internal and external stimuli
- denial can be an outcome of atypical depression
- Pride can prevent someone accepting they are unwell. As can fear.

Heal

Heal, so you don't ever have to
give a sarcastic tone
to uplifting messages.

Heal, so you never have to
make anyone else
the object of your
own frustration.

Heal, so when someone
tells you they love you,
you may allow yourself
to believe them.

"JUST
BECAUSE
NO ONE ELSE CAN
HEAL OR DO YOUR
INNER WORK FOR
YOU DOESN'T MEAN
YOU CAN, SHOULD,
OR NEED TO DO IT

ALONE"

— Lisa Olivera

can be helpful and healthy

- psychological discomfort due to an event or behaviour that is objectively wrong.

Or unhealthy

- same discomfort but due to unrealistic/high expectations

Facing healthy guilt
↳ take responsibility
↳ seek forgiveness
↳ change beliefs/behaviours to be in line with what is morally right
↳ heal the relationship

It is a very intense feeling of inadequacy, worthlessness and being flawed

Facing unhealthy guilt
↳ practice self-compassion
↳ reflect on standards/ expectations

A painful, internalised emotion that can lead to fear of rejection and potentially result in mental health issues

Shame can lead to reduced self-respect, and a decline in defining self-worth. It produces a negative sense of self if shame is prolonged

Seeking help to deal with shame can help by learning ways to practice self-compassion and how to accept imperfections

A personal response to self-criticism due to not being enough or doing things "wrong"

Breaking old routines, patterns and habits

Safe and healthy relationships

Improved ability to manage emotions

Commitment to recovery

Accomplishing goals

more open to change

Setting and maintaining boundaries

Self-validation

more stable appetite

Better able to deal with failure

healing
signs you are

resilience

Accepting Support

Seeking internal validation as well as external

forgiveness for yourself and others (when appropriate)

A more positive outlook

Acceptance

Self-responsibility

Reduced distress and negative emotion symptoms

recognise and manage triggers

Improved sleep

Able to express needs and thoughts

What I say to friends that are struggling

"How are you doing?"

"I've been thinking of you, I hope you are doing okay"

Sympathise

"I'm sorry you're going through that"

"make sure you prioritise your needs and wellbeing"

"that must be so tough"

"I'm so proud of you for being so strong"

"take time for yourself. don't over do it"

Listen

"I'm here for you"

"you'll get through this, and I'll be here for you the whole time"

"message me whenever"

comfort

"I'll be around if you want to do something"

"do what is going to be best for you"

Be available

- -

What I say to myself when I'm struggling

"you're wasting everyone's time"

"no one cares that you're struggling"

"you don't matter. Just grin and bear it. Don't let anyone down"

"you're pathetic"

"get out of bed. You're so lazy"

"you're broken. why can't you just get a grip and be normal?"

"people care because they're paid to"

"stop feeling sorry for yourself"

"other people have it so much worse"

"you are a disappointment"

"toughen up"

"grow up"

"this is all my fault"

"stop being so miserable"

"pull yourself together"

"I'm weak"

200

mindful moment

On the days when i feel a little bit okay, and i want to try to improve my mental health, i try using mindfulness. i ground myself, and notice the little things...

Do a body scan and notice any sensations on or inside your body

Bird song

The euphoria of cold water

Notice the colours in the sky

The smell after it rains

The beauty of nature's colours and forms

The aroma of my morning coffee

5 Notice the 5 senses. What can i... Taste? Feel? Hear? Smell? see?

☮ Meditation ☮

♫ Your favourite song or album ♫

warm baths

Colours and Shades of my surroundings

The Scent of flowers

The feeling of grass or sand between your toes

What am i grateful for?

Focus on an activity without distraction 👍

Forgive yourself

The purity of animals

the taste + texture of my favourite food

Focus closely on an object. Such as the curves, texture, and colours of a leaf

Runner's high and the rhythm of my breath

[Journal your thoughts and feelings]

[Be mindful of your emotions]

[Establish a routine with sufficient sleep and rest]

[Reflect on what you are grateful for]

[Drink enough water]

[meditate]

[Have a healthy diet, not consisting of excessive sugar]

Make your mental health a priority

[Deep breathing]

[Avoid lots of social media]

[Communicate your needs]

[Reach out for support if needed]

[Go outside, for fresh air, exercise, and sunshine.]

[Be kind to yourself]

[Say 'no']

[Celebrate achievements]

[Take time to relax]

[listen to yourself and your needs]

Self soothe
using all 5 senses
- touch e.g. soft material
- taste e.g. sour or mint
- smell e.g. lavender
- sight e.g. calm image
- hear e.g. white noise

Emotional awareness
to identify and express feelings e.g. a list, art, or journal

- Meditation
- Grounding
- Breathing exercises

Create a crisis plan, with support sources

Distract, but don't let it become avoidance behaviour

problem-focused

MANAGE TIME

SEEK SUPPORT

PLAN AHEAD

TO-DO LISTS

ESTABLISH BOUNDARIES

WEIGH THE PROS AND CONS

emotion-focused

NO TECHNOLOGY

JOURNAL   LABEL THE FEELING   SEEK HELP

MINDFULNESS   POSITIVE THINKING

BREATHE   MEDITATE

MUSIC   COUNTING

Managing stress

WALK   ART

YOGA

READ

EXERCISE   JOURNAL

SEE FRIENDS

PLAY A GAME

Connect to your values

Opposite action
consistent and positive

- Affirmations and inspirations
- Something calm
- Humour e.g. a comedy movie

Healthy coping mechanisms

Self care

Track positive habits

A DAY IN THE LIFE

As Heraclitus famously stated, 'change is the only constant in life'. So although each day looks different, there are a few things that almost always the same. Mental illness doesn't take a day off, however hard I try.

EARLY.

- Wake up some time between 3:30 and 5:30 am

Morning

- Get up when my alarm goes off, even though I've been lying awake for at least an hour and a half

- Coffee to fuel all the tasks and anything I now regret planning. Medication.

- Take time to summon energy and willingness to do the day

Afternoon

- Exhausted by approximately 2pm due to 12+ hours of worrying
- Nap or emotionally disconnect until I can go back to bed
- Try to do everyday things, become overwhelmed physically and mentally, then resent myself for failing at being human

Evening

- Very tired, likely grumpy as hanger sets in following little to no lunch due to nausea from stress, and not wanting to eat

- Dinner. slightly revived

- Chill to cool my mind before sleep

- Medication for sleep and to stop nightmares. Doesn't stop nightmares

Reminders

No situation is worth your mental health. You can leave a place or person.

Be gentle. Be kind. Everyone is battling things you may not know about.

It's okay to take a break, to give yourself time, recharge, and come back stronger than before.

Take care of your homes:
- Your body
- Your mind
- The Earth

Now is not forever

You can be kind and still say no. You can still be a work in progress and love yourself too.

Mental health Struggles

are	are not
Important	A sign of weakness
A priority	
Real	A decision or choice
Complex	
Part of being human	The same for everyone
Changeable	Shameful
Relevant for everyone	Taboo
linked to physical health	Manipulation tactics
Inconsistent	For attention
On a continuum	Easy

The difference between coffee and your opinion is that I asked for coffee

love isn't a prize, it's a feeling

Be kind. Always.

Allow yourself to bloom

Make someone's day

22/08

LET GO OF WHAT ISN'T HELPFUL

Self-criticism

failure ⟶ a lesson learned

selfish ⟶ self-care

weak ⟶ trying

emotional ⟶ self-aware

too... ⟶ enough

Negatives

'I'm always late' ⟶ 'Thank you for waiting'

cheer up ⟶ feel your emotions

never quit ⟶ sometimes the only option is to walk away

Hide upset ⟶ It's okay to not be okay

Dismissal

I should / have to ⟶ I'm trying and doing my best

Just grin and bear it ⟶ what can I change or control?

It could be worse ⟶ my pain is valid

You'll be fine in the end ⟶ I'm here to support you through this

Toxic positivity

You'll be fine ⟶ It's okay if you need to seek help

You're perfect or a failure ⟶ be patient and kind with yourself

Don't be negative ⟶ It's normal to feel negative emotions

Its probably not that bad ⟶ validate

Stay positive ⟶ work through challenges

YOU CAN DO THIS

Have a kind heart, fierce mind & brave spirit

Make yourself a priority. You can't pour from an empty cup

The sun will rise again

life is tough but so are you

Distress tolerance skills

STOP

Stop   Take a step   Observe   Proceed
        back   mindfully

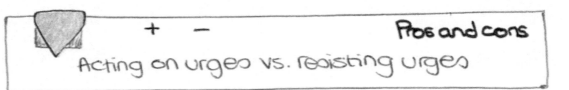

+   —   Pros and cons

Acting on urges vs. resisting urges

Distracting with ACCEPTS

Activities   Contributing   Comparisons   Emotions

Pushing away   Thoughts   Sensations

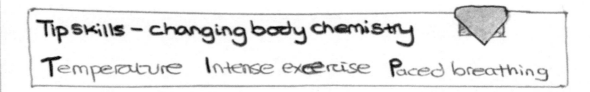

Tip skills — changing body chemistry

Temperature   Intense exercise   Paced breathing

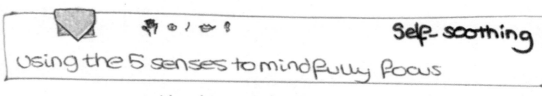

Self-soothing

using the 5 senses to mindfully focus

Marsha M. Linehan

For more information and detail → DBT skills training handouts and Worksheets

Love

find your love language

· Quality time · Acts of service · Gifts · physical touch ·
· words of affirmation ·

Self-love

WHAT WE THINK

Something you "should" be doing

Something you "should" know how to do

IT IS...

WHAT IT

REALLY IS...

1 progress not perfection
2 setting boundaries
3 understanding your needs
4 self respect
5 showing up for yourself
6 investing in yourself
7 addressing negative thinking
8 seeking help if needed
(mental health, physical health, career, relationship, emotional)

Strengthening relationships

· Respect differences in opinion
· Validate emotions
· Avoid passive aggressive comments/behaviours

· Use 'I' statements in disagreements to reduce blame
· face challenges as a team
· Acceptance that no relationship is perfect

· Listen
· learn to understand them
· put effort in
· focus on the facts
· be gentle
· show an interest

If Physical health problems were treated like mental health problems

I'm not sure you're trying to get over your flu

Get over it

It's all in your head

You look fine

You'll be okay in the morning

You have no reason to be injured

It's only a break, you'll be alright

Try to not have a heart attack

Other people have it so much worse

Are you trying to get rid of your diabetes?

Cheer up, and your illness will go away

Consider yourself lucky

How can you be unwell when you have/are...

Stay positive, have a positive attitude and you'll be alright

At least pretend you don't have food poisoning

It could be worse

HEALTH

Have you tried not having a broken arm?

High blood pressure? Just relax

being unwell or hurt, but not enough to get help or support.

No cure, you have to live like this from now on

But you're so — (positive adjective)_, how can you have this disease?

Distract yourself from your broken ankle and you'll be fine after a while

Should I tell people I am in hospital? Should I tell my friends I'm sick?

Can you not wait until after ____ to have flu?

But you've had help, why can't you run yet?

Give it time, your bone will heal. It can't be broken forever

Don't mention your tooth ache at a job interview

don't just lie about all day

It's not healthy to take medication to treat diabetes. It's not natural

This virus is your fault

Just change your perspective

Types of rest

Time away / a holiday

a quiet, peaceful mind   Sleep

Quality time   presence in the
with loved ones   moment, without
                      thinking about the
unscheduled   past, or worrying
time   about the future

engage with an "unproductive" activity

time alone

a break from
expectations

Stillness

permission
to not help
someone

Immersion in
the arts or
nature

Safety and
quiet

'You're not a victim for sharing your story. You are a survivor setting the world on fire with your truth. And you never know who needs your light, your warmth and raging courage.'   - Alex Elle

The negative cycle can be broken in different parts by different types of therapy

Feelings ↔ Thoughts
Thoughts ↔ physical symptoms
Behaviours

Healthy life balance

Achieve · Connect · enjoy (A C E)

Stress occurs due to an imbalance of resource and demand

Improve the moment: Use Imagery, find meaning, and purpose, relax, focus on one thing, vacate, encourage

Key Therapy Points

Relationships:
- Attachment types
  ○ Avoidant
  ○ enmeshed
  ○ Secure
  ○ Disorganised

- 4 types of closeness
  ○ emotional
  ○ physical
  ○ Sexual
  ○ mental / intellectual

communication styles:
- passive
- aggressive
- direct aggressive
- indirect aggressive

The 5 basic needs
• Belonging   • Nurtured
• Protected   • supportive
• Limits and boundaries

Boundaries
• physical   • emotional
• Sexual   • Intellectual

Trauma = emotional Shutdown
↳ Acute, chronic, complex
↳ crossed boundaries + adverse childhood experiences likely cause

The ABCs of emotions:
• Pay Attention to the emotion
• where do I Feel it in my Body?
• Create an outlet for it

Fear response

Fight
Flight
Freeze

ACCEPTANCE

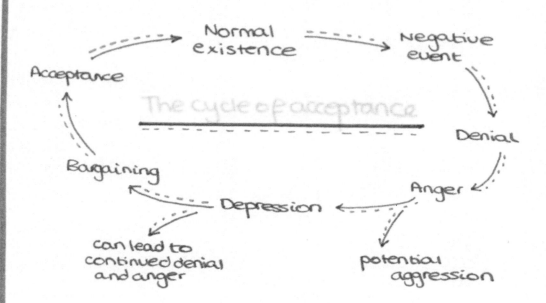

The cycle of acceptance

Normal existence → Negative event → Denial → Anger → Depression → Bargaining → Acceptance → Normal existence

Anger → potential aggression

Depression → can lead to continued denial and anger

Self-acceptance

'True self-acceptance shows up in that moment when you realise that peace cannot co-exist with war. The moment you choose to stop being your own enemy and to love yourself instead' - Rebecca Ray

- Recognise your imperfections
- Keep a list of reminders of your best attributes
- Avoid self-criticism
- love and accept your inner child

Radical acceptance

'we are all born so beautiful. The greatest tragedy is being convinced that we are not.'
- Rupi Kaur

- Accepting something without:
  ↳ judging it or yourself
  ↳ trying to forcefully change it
- Reflect on what it is I'm not able to accept e.g. an emotion or event
- Remember you aren't giving up, but bravely accepting when appropriate

216

Positive pin-ups

Be gentle with yourself

Grow through what you go through

Strive for progress, not perfection

Give yourself credit for never giving up

It's okay not to be okay

Make yourself a priority

You are stronger than your fears

remember how far you have come

There are only two things you can control in life:
1 your attitude
2 your effort

Don't wait for the storm to pass. Learn to dance in the rain

Shoot for the moon even if you miss you'll land among the stars

Believe in yourself and your ability

Little by little day by day what's meant for you will find it's way

YOU MATTER

you're not alone ♡

You are ENOUGH

Life has its ups and downs

You have survived every single bad day

THE PAST

NOW

WHAT IF?

BE BRAVE

Remember how far you've come

let go of what weighs you down

over-preparing

avoid eye contact

Neglect my needs

people pleasing

self-criticism

Avoid conflict

Not leave home

tidying

expecting too much from myself

Avoiding phone calls

Not trust

Overthinking

being anxious

Ruminate over the past

Over-apologising

Avoiding unknown events and places

Not interacting with others

Writing lists

Organising

re-watching comforting TV shows

distract my mind by multitasking

bite my nails

making assumptions

Things I do because of....

Staying in bed

Isolate from others

lie to others

Put others first

Stay at home

punish myself

Not wanting to get out of bed

restrictive eating

deny myself what I need

Listen to music to block out reality

Seek comfort

Cry

Silence

Self harm

sleep

over-compensate with forced "happiness"

being depressed,

Not commit to occasions

numb my feelings

Think about life/death

Be quiet

Self-hatred

ignore my needs

Not getting dressed

avoid responsibilities

Not keep up good health physically

Avoid activities

Self-criticism

I'm 16, being assessed in A + E by the triage nurse. By this point I have been self-harming on a frequent basis, but this time I had shared with a teacher that I didn't want to be alive any more. So I'm taken to hospital by my parents. After checking my vitals, the nurse addresses my cut wrist. 'Superficial' was her comment, with a strange air of disappointment. I was then taken to the children's ward for the night as the psychologist wasn't able to see me until the morning. I curled up in a ball, holding myself and hoping I could fold so small that I would disappear. The beeps of all the equipment that tiny children were attached to tormented me. I felt like a fraud for being there, just because I was a bit sad. But I was in pain too, its just that no one could see it. The invisibility of mental illness, except when it can manifest as physical signs, is an ongoing difficulty when it comes to validating and taking the issue seriously. The danger in this denial or insufficient concern when it comes to mental illness is the need to demonstrate emotional suffering. Not understanding or not being able to verbalise the feeling leaves only being able to show it. But the associated risk is huge. At 16 I didn't understand the complexity of what I was experiencing, couple that with being disregarded, my only outlet was self destruction to my body so i could ignore the emotional pain. 9 years later, at the time of writing, I am only slightly closer to knowing what's going on. I can now describe how i feel. but can't identify or deal with emotions very well. I have a dauntingly long way to go yet.

healthy love

- occasional disagreements, that are calmly resolved with respect for one another
- Apologising when appropriate
- Having and maintaining personal boundaries
- Acceptance of the other's imperfections
- communicate discomfort or concerns
- mutual respect, vulnerability, and support
- Able to express individuality
- Not seeking unconditional love

unhealthy love

- unwilling to apologise for wrongdoings
- unneccesarily raising their voice
- Not having independence or interests outside the relationship
- Lying to keep peace / avoid conflict
- Always taking your partner's advice
- No boundaries
- Prioritising the needs of the other
- Taking responsibility for their actions. either positive or negative

Sleep

Sleep and mental health

worry/stress → disturbed sleep → tiredness → difficulty with daily life → low self-esteem → worry/stress

- Insomnia (difficulty falling asleep or staying asleep or waking early)
- Issues that disturb sleep e.g. panic attacks or nightmares

Tips to improve Sleep

- Nightime routine
- No screens for at least an hour before bed
- Meditation
- Avoid caffeine in the late afternoon

- Practice gratitude
- weighted blanket
- Ambient sounds, white noise or music
- Busy day to induce tiredness

- CBD products
- Reading
- Essential oils
- Bath

Long term sleep issues can lead to...

- Relationship problems
  - ↳ irritable : arguments
  - ↳ tiredness can reduce effort input

- Struggles in maintaining a social life
- Feeling hungrier. Reliance on caffeine
- vulnerability to mental health issues
- difficulty carrying out daily tasks

Reasons why people with depression might sleep a lot

- Exhaustion
  - ↳ from pressures
  - ↳ from pretending to be okay
  - ↳ as a symptom

- For safety from themselves
- Not wanting to be bombarded with negative thoughts and self-criticism
- medication

- Avoidance
- Insomnia at night that results in tiredness so can encourage napping in the day
- physical fatigue

What an emotion may be hiding

Emotion	Possible meaning
Sadness	repressed anger
Anger	Crossed boundaries
Guilt	Letting others define how to behave
Anxiety	Lack of reassurance
Disappointment	Unrealistic expectations
Grief	Shows what is important to you

Behind this...

ANGER

Could be...

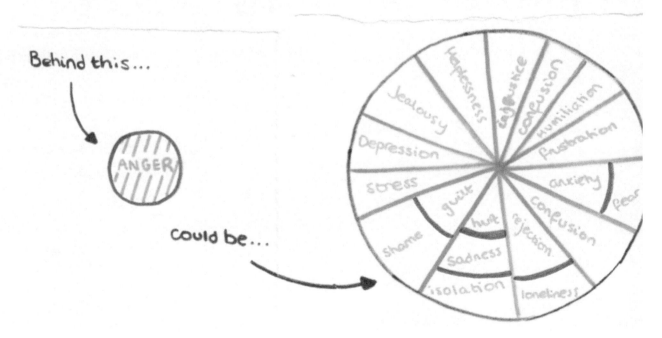

NO PAIN.

I used to be quite a good hockey player.
One of the things that made me good
was how "tough" I was. I could do
multiple training sessions per day, had
the right amount of aggressive for
a "non-contact" sport, and was always
getting injured in the name of sport. I
endured concussions, broken bones, a
split-open forehead, all because I was
willing to put my body on the line for
my team. But behind this apparent
bravery was a soul so damaged that
it offered up the physical body to
destruction, because that's what it
felt it deserved. The positive reinforce-
ment of praise for suffering and all
the wins we got, meant I saw no
logical or emotional reason to
stop. Until I snapped.

NO GAIN.

The mental and emotional resilience required to compete at a high level had mostly alluded me. Despite the input of a sports psychologist, I was no good at handling the pressure. The older I got the more this had an impact. It seemed to happen overnight, my spirit for the game suddenly collapsed. The physical toll it took didn't seem worthwhile any longer, and my love of being part of a team went too. The need to trust and rely on other people had shattered in my mind, I couldn't do it anymore. I was so damaged in every aspect of my life and personality, but it had always just been hockey and nothing else mattered. But now, without it, nothing mattered. I hadn't noticed my decline until it became all-consuming and I fell apart. I dropped out of uni, moved back home, and began a downward spiral of feeling like a failure as well as desperately sad. I tried to cope on my own, then covid hit and I was all I had to rely on. Then as we gradually had to participate in life again, I broke down. ~~Cuxsbsda~~ Cue inpatient psych admission.

- Trying to control others
- acting in a way that doesn't align with your values
- making comparisons with others
- Avoidance e.g. people, places, or emotions.
- Resisting change
- Social isolation
- making excuses

Self-Sabotage

- Not accepting compliments or praise

- Not saying 'no'
- Self-criticism
- excusing others' harm towards you
- not keeping your boundaries

- pushing people away or becoming overly-attached/dependent on others

- Isolating when you are hurting

- opening up when not appropriate

- putting the needs of others above our own

Why?
- expectation of pain
- Fear of the past repeating
- Not feeling worth your own respect or care
- avoiding support

- perfectionism
- Staying in a physically or emotionally abusive environment
- Not prioritising my own needs
- Apologising for who you are
- needing external validation

I miss you

I miss you
and your nips with baby teeth
accidents in house training
naughty antics, chewing holes

Your hair. Everywhere.

I miss your smell
your loving gaze
sympathetic licks
wagging tail. Always.
I miss you just knowing
when I needed you
to do nothing
or play
or cuddle
I miss falling asleep
with you just there
always by my side
I miss
your chin on the table
your huffs. You knew best.
I miss fun
in the snow
in the sea.
I miss your soul.
But I have the memories,
and your little damson tree.

I don't know you yet

You pass by me
in shop windows
I catch your eye
you smile back
I don't know you yet

I recieve all your mail
celebrate your birthday
But
I do not know you

Your face
is in my passport
we've been
to the same places
How have we never met?

There is a 17 year old
a stranger
on my driving license
I don't know her yet

we like the same
books
music
films
yet you're a stranger

I tidy up
after you
cook for you
But who are you?

I pay for your
haircuts
I do your nails
choose your clothes
You ignore me

I've seen you
in my family phones
You're smiling
we've not
been introduced

You leave
nasty comments
notes that hurt
I don't even know you

I think of you
we share memories
thoughts and fears
Tell me who you are

You message my friends
talk to my family
How do they know you?

I think people like you
So maybe
I should give you
a chance

Watering can

I am a watering can
Heavy
with the weight
of water, imposed
on me by others
or by chance
from rain.

It holds me down
Sometimes overflows
but only a little
Still full
to the brim.

I rely on safe hands
to unbalance me
Only enough
to let the water flow.
Then they hold me,
keep me balanced.
Nearly all the water
is gone.

The rain nozzle
Controlled
natural.
manageable.
Few can cope with
the singular,
uncontrolled flow.
But they are the best,
allowing a quicker
more powerful
release.

But there is potential
to cause damage.
I am a watering can.
Often overlooked,
in favour
of the easy-going,
reliable hose.

I can't release
in numerous healthy
ways, adapting
to perform
as needed.

I spill,
make a mess.

But hoses,
they're restrained.

But sometimes,
the can is perfect,
reminding me,
I'm a watering can.
Not a watering can't.

Hurting

I'm hurting now
Right this second
I don't know how
To not beckon
Pain when I'm sad
I feel so trapped
I could go mad
The scars I've mapped
Along my wrist
Showing my pain
'stop.' you insist
What do I gain
It's all I have
What more is there?
stopping isn't fair
Darkness still here
Haunting my mind
Fills me with fear
Not at all kind
I feel myself lose
My blood runs cold
I can't refuse
my heart rate drops
my body slows
The hurt numbs me
That's when pain shows
And I can see
What is hurting
It is my heart
Ideas flirting
Tear me apart
Torn between them

Bad ideas
Better than numb
But feel my fears
If I do it
I have control
or I could sit
Try to feel whole
But its missing
I've lost my soul

It's so much more

Depression is so much more
Than sadness
It's crying so much you don't think
It will ever stop
It's waking each morning
And dreading the day
It's a heavy darkness
That sits in your chest
It's an exhaustion
No amount of sleep will conquer
It's a hollow emptiness
That is left behind
After your soul has drained away
It's an ache that engulfs
Your whole body
It's a complete loss of happiness,
motivation, and spirit
It's a pain that makes life feel
questionable
It's a threat to all that you are
It's so much more
Than sadness

Fall

Never.
Not once.
Did you want me
To fly.
But only to fall.
For you.

Don't

I don't sleep
I don't eat
I don't rest
I don't stop
I don't smile
I don't know
I don't commit
I don't promise
I don't laugh
I don't confess
I don't tell the truth
I don't feel safe
I don't feel happy
I don't feel at all
I don't know who I am
I don't care

Hands

I hold my head
In my hands
But really
it is I that wants to be held
My heart
to be cradled
In steady hands
My soul
To be nurtured
And my mind
To be protected
But instead
All I can do
Is hold my head
In my hands

GONE

One day
I'll be gone.
I've really
tried hard.
But it's been
a while.
Since the
sun shone

The positives

You say
Focus
On the positives
But
there's
too many
clouds
Their edges
Blurred.
I can't see
Any silver linings

Therapy

You've made me cry
More than anyone has
You've made me vulnerable
You know my secrets
I love to hate you
And hate that I love you

Panic attack

My chest is heavy
The panic attack
Kneals on my ribcage
Hands around my neck
I cannot breathe
The pressure builds
Behind my eyes
Pushing from within
Nausea surges
Through my abdomen

My body becomes weak
I rest my head back
against the wall
close my eyes
Try to breathe

cold coffee

I sit
I wait
Patiently
Finally
You remember
You hold me
I've gone cold
Not quite
Iced coffee
cool
popular
refreshing
but tepid
you struggle
through
with me
I'm bitter
but that's
now me
cold coffee

Little bird

I am a bird
with a broken wing
I cannot fly
I cannot sing
I only cry
Here in my cage
Even if I could
spread my wings
and fly away
I'm trapped
so here I stay

The pain,
How it burns,
How the blood runs.
Relief
For a moment.
I Forget
The Ache
In my heart,
The darkness
In my mind.

235

A poem I wrote while in hospital:

A dose, a day

I'll start
Where every day starts
The medication queue
White light
through frosted glass
Staring at my toes
hoping no one speaks.
A rainbow of pills
in their paper thimble.
My neck snaps back
down in one.
A sip, then speak
Proof you've swallowed.
Then coffee
My order known
before I ask
I've been here too long.
With each new face
I think that.
Why can't I cope yet?
Why aren't I okay yet?
Outside
I sit, sip
caffeine animates my brain
energises my veins.
To therapy
as little

or as much
as I feel
I can do today.
Groups.
Sharing.
Supporting.
Emotions so strong
they're almost
visible.
In the air
Some slow. Heavy.
Some speed
around the room.
Pent up
finally free
Release is new
emotions naïve
they know not
what they are.
nor do I.
lunch is light
pain
certainly wins
your appetite.
More therapy,
if your mind allows.
Then enough.
Enough for today.

Alone

I pace
back and
forth
when I'm alone
I punch
solid
walls
when I'm alone
I cry
forever
it seems
when I'm alone
I cut
my poor
wrists
When I'm alone
I think
into
oblivion
when I'm alone
I dream
how to
die
when I'm alone
I take
off the
mask
when I'm alone
I am
who I
am
when I'm alone

I write
how
I feel
when I'm alone
I'm more
okay
(just)
when I'm alone
I'm lonely
and
I'm scared
when I'm alone
I know
only how
to be alone

237

Rest

Why do you not
care that I'm sad?
You turn away
make me feel bad
Am I too much?
Best to ignore.

In case I break
From one small
touch.
But that's not
fair
It's not my fault
I need your care
Don't ignore me
My heart
will tear.

I'll lose myself
You'll lose me too
I've really tried
To see it through
Life's a test
One I've failed.
It's for the best

Everyone wins
If I can rest.

Pain

what more can I do?
I've tried to get through.
I've made it so clear
That I live in fear
I've told who I should
I've done what I could
But I'm still alone
I can't stand your tone
Instead I will hide
All the times I've cried
Cover up my pain
Pretend I am sane
It's all I have left
Victim of a theft

my hope
disappeared
Just as I had
feared
No options
remain
But to live
In pain

Trying

You want
to know
why I hide
The truth
And always lie
You can't get
Just how sad
I am, and yet
You don't try
To know
Maybe
Sometimes but
always? No.
You can't
relate
But please
I need patience
Just wait
I'm really
trying
It seems you
forget,
leaves me crying

Sleep

Once my weary eyes fall shut
I want to fall asleep, but...
My heart pounds loud in my chest
And my racing mind won't rest

Sleep eludes me, I'm so tired
my thoughts are frantically fired
I want to dream, but can't rely
that nightmares won't creep in, sly.

Exhaustion will take over
but thoughts need going-over
to overthink, analyse.
What is truth and what are lies?

Finally, I fall asleep
Worries stay, they're mine to keep.
They stick around and won't budge
They taunt me, and hold a grudge.

I really hope that one day
the bad thoughts will go
then I can sleep, and be okay.

'part of her mystery
is how she is calm
in the storm and
anxious in the
quiet'

    - Jm Storm

You'll silently bloom,
beautifully
in your own way.

- Dhiman

Suffering in silence

It is absolutely terrifying
the kind of deep suffering
the happiest looking people
are able to hide inside
themselves

    - Nikita Gill

'It is not the bruises
on the body that hurt
It is the wounds of
the heart and the
scars on the mind'

    - Aisha Mirza

'perhaps if tearful little
boys were comforted
instead of shamed
there would not be
so many angry men
struggling to express
& empathise with
emotions'

    - Leila Schott

It's not as if
I didn't try. But
somewhere between
being who you needed and
being who I needed, I
became a stranger
to us both

    - BMM

239

wild. Caged.

Wild
unfamiliar
with the ways
of the world
I am kept
in a cage
Four walls

Lies
Fear
Trauma
Pain
A cage
of my design
"my fault"
But you
gave the tools
provided the walls
Now
I am trapped
You say
I put myself
in this cage
But no
I was
cornered
Terrified
Confused
I Backed
into my cage
I try
I lash out
I cry
You scould

You blame
The cage
is all I have
So
I sit
defeated
in my cage
You hold the key
I cannot
escape
I am wild
caged
A cage for life
For life a cage

It's like
Gasping for air
After swimming
Too deep
Relief
Washes over me
Like the waves
All around
Trying to
Stay afloat
But I ache
I'm exhausted
I won't
Seek a lifeguard
they'll say
I'm fine
I haven't drowned
Not yet
But I am
can't you see?

I wish I was stronger than this

I wish I was braver than this

I wish I could speak up

I wish I could stand up
for myself

I wish I could cope
more than this

I wish I was better

than this.

Depression destroys
Each and every
Part of who you are.
Really gets it's claws in,
Engulfing your entire being.
Some days are tough,
Some days are unbearable.
In constant pain.
Ongoing distress.
Needless to say, it's shit.

I'm trying
Can't you see?
Desperately
Trying
To save me

The eyes
They say
Are
The Window

To the soul
No wonder
Mine are blue

I have
2 types
of colors...

Calm

- peaceful
- quiet
- relaxed
- myself
- productive
- independent
- motivated
- hard working
- self-reliant
- mindful
- comfortable
- reflective
- deep thinking
- controlled
- mellow

Self-destruct

- negative
- scared
- emotional
- on edge
- helpless
- despair
- harmful
- uncontrolled
- irresponsible
- dangerous
- isolated
- risky
- lonely
- irrational
- erratic
- unpredictable
- impulse
- reckless

Putting the work in

What I...

want	vs.	need
to avoid negative emotions		to recognise and sit with negative emotions
perfection		acceptance of imperfections
to be heard and understood		make my feelings and needs known

distress tolerance skills

- Stop. physically. don't move. Take a step back. Notice. Observe. Inside and outside the body. Proceed mindfully
- engage wholly in an activity
- identify and label the emotion, without judgement
- Safe expression e.g. artwork

Start of the week :

priorities for the week, to do less _____ , to do more _____ , I would like to feel _____ , to do that I will _____

End of the week :

I felt _____ this week, I'm grateful for _____ , I achieved _____ ,
I forgive _____ , I needed _____

Recognising a decline in mental health

- Feeling exhausted and heavy
- isolating
- disorganised
- panic attacks
- easily upset
- self doubt
- loss of motivation
- coping mechanisms don't work as well
- lack of focus
- self criticism
- sleeping too much/little
- dissatisfaction
- over or undereating
- Procrastination
- withdrawn

Prioritise my needs and make them known :

- I can ask for help
- not compromising myself
- not changing for others
- keep my boundaries
- process my emotions
- work on internal validation

My mental health bucket list

- [ ] No longer compromise myself to please others
- [ ] Prioritise myself and my mental health
- [ ] Accept that I'm only human and will make mistakes
- [ ] Maintain my boundaries
- [ ] Not let fear stop me doing things
- [ ] No longer avoid my feelings
- [ ] Stop apologising when I've done nothing wrong
- [ ] Seek more internal validation
- [ ] No longer disregard my needs or values in order to avoid conflict
- [ ] Use more therapy skills
- [ ] Allow myself to trust and be vulnerable

I WONDER WHAT IT'S LIKE...

- To wake up and look forward to the day
- To eat and not worry how fat it'll make you
- To not regret everything I've ever done or said
- To not overthink and overanalyse conversations and events
- To not hate yourself
- To be upset talking or thinking about self harm and suicide
- To have self confidence
- To sleep without nightmares
- To not worry about EVERYTHING
- To trust people
- To not feel alone
- To be happy

proud

I'm so proud of you.
I'm proud that you keep showing up,
every, single, day. I'm proud of all
the tough decisions you had to
make and that even though it was
hard, you stood your ground. I'm
proud that you never gave up on
yourself and kept fighting for
everything you love. I'm proud that
despite everything you've been
through, you still wake up and
find ways to smile every day.
I'm proud that even though you've
seen so much darkness, you
always search for the light.
I'm proud of you and how far
you've come, and I'm even more
excited for everything
that's coming next.

- Nikki Banas

An open letter:

Thank you, to all those who have saved me. Especially on the days I didn't want to be saved. On the days that I have felt most alone, most in need of a shoulder to cry on, and gentle arms to be held in. Thank you for being there. For all the times I have cried myself to exhaustion, worried myself into silence, fallen into despair, thank you for holding my hand through it all. Thank you for never giving up on me, even though I gave up on myself. You believed in me, saw the strength I thought I'd lost, and stood by me as I found it again. Thank you for pushing me, even when I resisted. I thought you wanted me to fall, but really you were helping me to fly. Thank you for persevering with me, when I was at my worst, and it would be so easy to walk away. You dragged me back from the dark, and showed me the light. Thank you, for saving my life.
All my love,
Jenna
x

Printed in Great Britain
by Amazon